Mind Twisters

MIND TWISTERS

ERNEST TOTTOSY

Translator and Collaborator
for the English Version
HELEN M. SZABLYA

Copyright © 1987
Dr. Ernest Tottosy and Helen M. Szablya.

All rights, including translation, film, electronic, serial and all subsidiary rights, belong to the author and the translator.

ISBN: 1-4781-6817-X
ISBN-13: 9781478168171

TRANSLATOR'S NOTES

Three years ago I did not know Dr. Ernest Tottosy. I still have not met him in person and yet, it seems like I have always known him. Through the moving account of his prison ordeal, going with him into the deep abyss of madness and back again — he became a brother. Granted, we came from the same kind of background, yet there is more to this feeling of kinship than mere circumstances. His beautiful soul gives life to the story; while reading the book we are with him and get to know him intimately. This was much more so when, in the process of translating the manuscript, I had to relive the events with him in order to portray them accurately.

I had a tremendous helper in this task: my daughter-in-law, Marcey Painter Szablya. She went through every word and scrutinized every sentence with the precision of a playwright. As an American she became acquainted with the sad fate of Hungary through our son, Janos, who had escaped with us as a two and a half year old. Marcey and I had just completed the researching, writing and the production of the oral history drama, "Hungary Remembered," about the Hungarian Revolution of 1956. "Mind Twisters" was one of the more than a hundred stories used in this oral history drama. Marcey had the perfect background to do the editorial revisions for "Mind Twisters."

Next I would like to thank Dominique Mary (Niki) Szablya, my youngest daughter, and Marguerite Perner, two beautiful young people, who entered all the corrections into the word processor, while adding their own observations. Last, but not least, we owe a debt of gratitude to Caroline Berry for doing the last tedious proofreading of the manuscript.

I sincerely hope that all the readers will appreciate this book as much as we did while we put our best efforts into making this important document available to the English-speaking public.

March 15, 1987

DIAGNOSIS OF AN INDUCED SCHIZOPHRENIA

In November, or maybe the end of October in 1953, I waited for the trial of my "conspiracy" case at the Marko Street Court in Budapest, Hungary.

Every day brought more prisoners to our cell. The 17th or 18th prisoner shoved into our cell in the early afternoon, looked 35. He had tiny eyes and a moustache. The prisoner in charge of our cell, questioned him. He answered with caution. After meals he crossed himself betraying his religion. This is how I met Ernest Tottosy for the first time.

Soon we became friends. I told him I had been arrested in my third year of medical school. He whispered his questions: was I acquainted with pharmacology? He recounted an incredible sequence of events that had just happened to him. For months his captors brought his food separately and the guards stayed with him until he finished eating. They were regularly feeding him some drug. He had visions, he heard voices, he could control neither his behavior nor his emotions. He confessed everything to the investigators, starting with his childhood pranks, all the way through the details of his "conspiracy." Shocked, I listened to some of his amazing adventures: the colorful vision of the Battle of Mohacs — an infamous defeat of the Hungarian Army by the Turks in 1526 — the description of the Great Voice "directing" him, the compulsion to tell the truth, and his "I have to tell all" behavior, a virtual suicide under the circumstances. He suffered this desperate state of mind for more than seven months. At that time I knew next to nothing about hallucinogenic alkaloids. I was not alone in my ignorance. The effects of LSD and other such drugs, were largely unknown in those days.

"Some day I might be able to write the entire story," Ernest said ...

... he put the finished manuscript in front of me in Geneva, 1983.

"I wrote every detail in the late fifties, but I had no time to make it into a story for the public," he said. "Now you know more about psychology as well as drugs. The whole world knows now that troublesome dissidents, like General Grigorenko, Bukovszki, Plius and many others, are locked into mental hospitals in the Soviet Union. I thought I could finally publish my memoirs of those days in 1952-1953. I would like to hear your opinion."

As a psychiatrist I find his account of his case history startling. The reader can follow the splitting of the conscious, the formation of the double identity, the tearing in two of a cohesively thinking and acting individual.

It is a detailed testimony of a witness to the extent that it makes even the psychiatrist stop and think. He portrays perfectly the onset of hallucinations, the changing symptoms and their final disappearance.

As a rule, schizophrenics do not subsequently write down their symptoms in detail and certainly not with believable cohesiveness. As a matter of fact they shrink from even talking about it. They fear another hospitalization, brought on because of their openness. We know, and very often the schizophrenic patient too is aware of, the fact that this mental illness is not like chickenpox which one can contract only once in a lifetime. Rather, schizophrenia is a mental structure which makes it possible for the illness to flare up again and again. Schizophrenia, just like diabetes, requires constant medical supervision in order to keep the patient's condition under control. If a person does not have the schizophrenic mental structure his or her personality cannot split, no matter how difficult the trials and tribulations he or she must endure.

So, what happened to Ernest Tottosy?

Tottosy had no symptoms of schizophrenia before 1952, or after 1953. He is a balanced, happy person. The war, and the occupations of Hungary by different powers, educated him to become a concerned, dutiful Hungarian politician. He, like Vladimir Bukovszki, who spent many years in various Soviet mental institution-prisons, is an example of a poised, spiritually well-functioning person. His mental state thus can rightfully be described as an induced schizophrenia. The exact reason for the symptoms' onset will not be known until the authentic medical records are made available. We can only guess until then: was it Mescalin? LSD? Or some other secret chemical used by the AVH under the supervision of the Soviets?

We, the readers, face the same situation as a medical expert examining the patient. The illness — through the detailed description — develops in front of our eyes. This mental state, so easily followed in the book, will undoubtedly become the topic of research some day. I am afraid the experts of the future will have but a few such verified reports from real, live witnesses. They will have to work like anthropologists, piecing together from fragments the entire picture of the psychiatric abuses of our age. It is obvious that the investigating authorities used the help of medical specialists in selecting the drugs, as well as their use. Naturally, the participating doctor could tell us the most about the case. Perhaps some day such a testimony will surface.

I have not heard of a similar case, neither during the three years I spent in prison, nor during the almost 30 subsequent years. None of my prison-inmates had talked about anything remotely similar to this case. This also represents a puzzle. It is to be feared that the authorities, trying to extract a favorable testimony from the accused, used medical knowledge to artificially break the prisoners' resistance. We do not hear about these cases because the captors took care their victims did not survive their sentences, making certain outside confessions would not occur. In a similar case the fate of the Polish officers of Katyn only became known to the unbelieving world through Josef Czapsky, an officer who inadvertently happened to be hospitalized away from camp at that time.

It is very probable that Ernest Tottosy's story is not unique, but as an eyewitness account, it undoubtedly is. At the same time it is a brilliantly presented story through which the reader can look into how madness develops. It also serves as a documentary account of the last year of Stalin's rule, 1952-1953. The events perfectly depict the behavior of those in power at the time, of madmen, comparable only to the Dr. Mengeles of concentration camps, acting without inhibitions or scruples.

Palo Alto, March 19, 1985.
    Laszlo Luka M.D.
    Adjunct Professor of Psychiatry
    California State University, Hayward.

TWO ENCOUNTERS

Events have encounters as well as people.
I arrived in London dead-tired on a foggy March evening in 1961.
Hungarians in England celebrated the anniversary of their 1848 revolution. The usual reception after my talk exhausted me completely. I blended into the crowd of friends and strangers trying to find the right moment to go home — to my hotel.

As I was leaving a stranger came up to me. I dreaded his run-of-the-mill questions, but I had to stop. I didn't quite catch his name.

"You have a very unusual family name. I just had to talk to you, although I know, you must be tired," he said for openers.

"Not at all..."

"Did you have any relatives who were arrested by the secret police?" his eyes searched my face as he asked.

"Of course. Before the revolution, including myself four male members of my family were political prisoners."

"Just like myself," he continued. "I lived through a nightmare at the Veszprem headquarters of the secret police. A prisoner was tortured for months and during that time he kept shouting your family name constantly. He must have been treated with drugs because doctors visited him all the time. Seemingly he went crazy... Did you know that relative of yours?"

"Yes."

"Did he become completely mad?... Did he die during the tortures?"

"None of the above... he is alive and well."

"Indeed?... And where, may I ask?"

I stopped for a minute. I had to smile while I answered:

"He is standing right in front of you. I was the one."

* * *

Fifteen years later, in 1976, the Atlantic Treaty Association held its usual general meeting in Coppenhagen.

The opening of the session at the Danish Parliament was over and I was walking towards the cafeteria with two Belgian friends. We were discussing the opening remarks of the Secretary General of NATO, Mr. Luns.

Suddenly an ascetic man faced me. He called me by name.

"My name is Rath. You knew me as "Mr. R." a long time ago. Do you remember me?

His face didn't ring a bell, but the mention of "Mr. R." did.

"I saw your name listed among those of the Belgian delegation," Mr. R. started. "I have been looking forward to this meeting for a long time."

His razor-edged face showed the signs of the past twenty-five years. Back in 1952 we wanted to escape together to Austria. Last time I saw him was at the Veszprem headquarters of the Hungarian secret police; I had shaken in my boots as they stared at us. He had been wearing a loosely fitting Soviet-style uniform of the Hungarian Army.

"I was always as thin as a rail," he said, reading my mind. "I could not gain any weight, ever. My only problem not caused by the secret police... they are responsible for everything else. Even for my being here."

"You don't like it here?"

"I do... I have a good job at the royal library."

A couple of reporters interrupted our conversation for a short interview. As soon as they left, Mr. R. came straight to the point:

"In this day and age people like facts. You should get your story published."

"I started writing it in 1957, right after I got out of prison, when everything was still fresh in my memory."

"Finish it fast," he pressed. "We are no longer young. We, who experienced it, have to explain the society of madmen to the others who haven't. Stalin's psychiatric prisons are still in use."

"True," I said. "And the mental agony is worse than the physical. The psychiatric poisons used by the secret police today in Communist countries were well known to the Indians of Peru and Mexico. They used these poisons to make their victims confess, or to drive them into madness and occasionally into death. The Indians named their poison mescalin, we now call it scopolomin."

"How many were made to confess with this method?" he asked.

"I have no idea. We'll never even know the number of victims, who remained mad after the treatment. Before the 1956 revolution there must have been at least a hundred so-called 'madmen' at the 'Mental Health Department' of the Prison Hospital."

"What could have happened to them?"

"Who knows? They could've been poisoned, murdered, or they simply disappeared after the sudden liberation during the uprising..." I answered.

"You are lucky, you know. You were among them, as one of those 'madmen,' in the power of sadists — yet, you are here now, able to speak for the helpless.''

THE SOUP

September, 1952, two months after my arrest.

A guard tore open the door of my cell. He led me to a sparsely furnished interrogation room. A young civilian sat at the desk.

"Do you remember me?" was his first question.

Almost all my interrogators started our sessions with this question. Many of them must have trailed me while I was wanted. Did they honestly believe I would recognize them?

"No," I answered truthfully.

"Why are you shaking? Are you cold? Or afraid?"

"My nerves... especially since that last unfortunate incident..."

"What are you talking about? Let's hear it!"

I stopped shaking as I told him about the sergeant who borrowed my watch, then forgot to put it on the inventory of my personal belongings. In return he promised to smuggle a poem to my wife. It was a personal version of an old political poem dating back to the Turkish occupation of Hungary.

"Are you out of your mind?" my interrogator smiled. "You wanted to smuggle a poem out of here? Out of the secret police building? Don't you know that everything can be held against you here, even your poems? Nothing that is smuggled out of here is innocent. Let's get down to business," he said looking at his notes. "Tell me everything, but... I'm not kidding, I want... EVERYTHING!"

He must have pressed a button with his foot because, on cue, a tousle-haired girl entered and sat down at the typewriter. She gazed at me as if I was made of plaster.

"You've been interrogated at least ten times. Three times it was recorded. Now we'll do it again."

I turned to the blank face of the typist ready to repeat my last confession. I remembered every word. When I got to the point where Mr. Maros, the lawyer, got me in touch with Mr. "R", the interrogator raised his hand.

"Why do you always say Mr. 'R'? Who is he? Don't you know his name?"

"Mr. Maros didn't want to reveal it. The last time he called him 'Rein'."

"O.K. then. Write 'Rein', Comrade."

I continued with the story of my would-be-escape.

"When were the leather manufacturers, the Balazs's arrested?" he interrupted me.

"The day before we were supposed to leave. I met their host at the railroad station and immediately jumped on another train..."

"Did you guess you were wanted?"

"I was convinced."

"You still looked up Mr. Maros in Budapest. You dared to leave your hiding place?"

"Yes."

"What did Maros say then?"

"That Mr. 'R',... excuse me, Rein, had just left to see me to discuss the final details of our escape."

"Are you willing to tell that to Maros's face?"

"Yes!"

"Would you recognize Rein if we'd confront you with him?"

"Yes!"

I was certain Mr. Maros, as well as Mr. "R", would deny everything. I couldn't. The most important thing was to get away from the secret police, known as the AVH, and be tried by a judge. As long as the investigation was in the hands of the secret police everything else... many other things might be unearthed.

The typewriter clicked away.

He asked a few more questions about the dollars, then looked at me with high expectations:

"Do you have something else to say?"

"No."

He bent forward. His breath singed my face.

"I warn you! Think it over!" he threatened.

"I have nothing else to confess."

"O.K. ... That's your business. But remember! We can find out anything. Someday you will voluntarily tell us everything we want to know. Do you believe me?"

"I am aware of it," I answered shaking on the inside.

"You should be! You must know that you will confess. We have our ways. Mindszenty, your cardinal[1], also confessed... Everything... Even more. Do you understand?"

He dismissed me with a wave of his hand. The guard was already in the room. I left with a feeling of certainty that I was never going to see the district judge. They would not finish my "case" with the "attempted escape."

---

[1] Primate Cardinal Joseph Mindszenty was arrested December 26, 1949. His was the first showcase trial which he could never recall, but the trial was widely publicized by Hungarian authorities. He "confessed" to many groundless accusations under the influence of drugs. He was tried in the Marko Street Court on February 2, 1949 and sentenced to life imprisonment.

Four days passed. Nights, I tossed around without sleep. The interrogator's threats haunted me: "Mindszenty has also confessed.. We have our ways!"

On the fourth day a stocky sergeant took me to the prisoners' daily wash. I barely put water on my neck when he was already reprimanding me: "Hurry up... Doctor!" He put a sarcastic emphasis on "Doctor".

I tried to find a dry spot on the towel. He yelled at me again: "Don't be so finicky, damn it!"

I tried to open the cell door on my way back.

"Don't touch that door," he grunted. "WE open the door for such a gentleman as you are."

He stopped on the threshold.

"Let me warn you about some things," he said pushing his cap on one side. "From now on there will be a new order of things. First: you can only go to the bathroom when I let out everybody, all at once. Not whenever you feel like it, but, when I want it. Understand?"

"Yes."

"No walking around in your cell during the day. You'll sit on the edge of your cot in "attention". Do you know what that means?"

"I know."

"Have you ever been a soldier?"

"I have."

"In People's Republic times?"

"No, before the war."

"Well, anyway. You know what it means. You will sit on the edge of your cot, face towards the door, in "attention", all day. Understood?"

"Yes."

"You can walk only before taps. I will yell it. There'll be cell inspection before taps... Don't smile!"

I couldn't stand it without a smile. My cell was as empty as a tomb. There was nothing in it except for a coarse blanket. What good could an inspection do?

"Inspection. Understand?" The door thundered as he slammed it shut.

I received my usual breakfast. Black coffee with a small piece of bread. The chikory smoothed away the bitterness of the coffee and I greedily grabbed it every morning. An hour later as I was sitting in attention on my cot I felt the need to go to the bathroom.

I trusted that "bathroom time" would soon come. It didn't. Every minute brought worse pains that tore at my kidneys. I couldn't bear sitting for another minute. I had to get up and drag myself up and down in my cell. Someone knocked in another cell. He couldn't bear it either.

I hoped the guard would remember that human nature also had its own ways.

There was no answer to the knocking I had heard before. I started knocking myself. No answer whatsoever. Not a sound. Nothing moved.

More knocks came from every direction.

"Shut-up, mother-fuckers!" the guard yelled from his post, but did not move.

I knocked again. This time I was more aggressive.

He opened the door and stared at me with angry eyes: "What do you want?"

"I've got to go! Please, I can't hold it any more!"

"Damn it!... You're just used to being waited on hand and foot. Next time I won't open the door, no matter what you do."

He barely finished the lecture, when another guard came to get me. His boots hammered hard on the floor.

According to the rites of taking the prisoner for interrogation, he clicked handcuffs on my wrists and led me to the well-known room on the second floor.

The black-haired lieutenant, my usual interrogator, sat at the table. He didn't even look up as he commanded: "Sit down!"

I concentrated on my escape story, burying everything else deep in my mind, trying to forget.

"I will confront you with Mr. 'R'. He denies he wanted to escape," the lieutenant said, turning to the guard: "Bring him in, Comrade!"

The prisoner who entered was unshaved and white as death. His thin legs rattled around in his enormous black boots, worn grey with age. The Soviet-style Hungarian uniform hanging from his shoulders was wrinkled beyond recognition.

"Do you know him?" the lieutenant demanded.

I examined the face well. I met him once at a restaurant in Budapest. Mr. Maros, the lawyer, introduced him as Mr. "R", a man to be a "fellow-traveller" during our escape to the West. Now it seemed he was a soldier. He must have been out of his mind, trying to escape if he was a defector. What should I answer?

"I don't remember clearly!" I said, trying to avoid a clear-cut commitment.

"Of course not!" the lieutenant said sarcastically. "Then he was still in civilian clothes. But maybe you can remember that he was going to escape with you?"

"Maybe!"

"No! That is a certainty. Maros has conceded to it. Tell him to his face you have met him."

The pale face helped me out by begging: "Say it. I was Mr. 'R'."

"Maybe," I repeated. "There was a lot of smoke and many people in the restaurant. And then... this uniform."

"It confuses you that a member of the Army of the Hungarian People's Republic was going to escape with you?"

I did not speak any more.

When the guard took me back to my cell I wanted to shout for joy. They still had nothing against me, except my escape. The young interrogator was just firing shots in the dark, using empty threats. I hoped and prayed nothing "else" would turn up.

* * *

"Are you hiding something in your pillow?" The stocky sergeant asked, swinging his billy club. He performed the cell inspection, just as he had forewarned.

"No, sir!" I answered. That "pillow" he mentioned was a slightly raised portion of the wooden cot. A couple of days ago I hid a piece of sinew I managed to fish out of the Sunday soup, but I had consumed it the same night.

He probed the "pillow" with his billy club. Then he pointed towards the cellar window: "Have you tried it yet?"

"What?"

"To reach the window."

I was surprised he had enough sense to guess that. Indeed I tried to stretch towards the window, in vain.

"That window is too high!" I replied.

"You bet it is. Once a prisoner, an acrobat, managed to reach it. He even squeezed himself through it... only to be caught by the dogs in the courtyard. You haven't seen them yet?"

"Oh, yes I have."

"Hm!... When?"

"One of the sergeants once opened the window where the food was passed in and I saw an enormous German shepherd standing on its hind legs right in front of the window."

"They are for real, you know."

He scanned all the stones in the wall, glancing up and down.

"Last summer," he continued casually, "we had a little mishap while training them. My buddy and I were in the fields with some of these huge beasts. We saw a couple of young lovers. He wanted to test the dogs and yelled: 'Catch them!'' One of the animals bit off the young man's hand from the wrist."

I didn't answer. He was examining the ceiling.

"We have the same kind of dogs on the border, too. They would've caught you good."

He made a few steps, then stared at my shoes: "Take them off!" He took my shoes and noticed the little iron half-moons, put there to protect the heels. He knocked them off by hitting the shoes against the wooden cot then put them in his pocket. I stood barefeet. My socks had long ago disintegrated during my imprisonment.

"Here," he threw my shoes back at me. "Now, show me your pockets!" He searched them thoroughly, but found nothing. Then he stopped in the middle of the cell and sized me up. "Aren't you afraid of Executioner Bogar?"

His question shocked me.

"I haven't done anything as serious as that..."

"Who knows? Where do you think your case is going to be tried?"

"I don't know." Indeed I didn't. The fact that I was a lawyer made no difference. Neither the letters of the law, nor my juridical sense, not even the way I was being examined gave me a clue. I no longer dared to hope for a trial at the District Court, charged with a simple escape case. I dreaded being taken to Budapest, to the secret police headquarters for further investigation.

"Aren't you afraid of Council Chairman Olti?" He was known to conduct the worst political trials. It was not a comforting feeling to look forward to being tried by the Judge presiding over the Mindszenty case. The guard did not even expect an answer. He went on with his tirade: "I don't want to see you scratch anything on the walls. Not the date, not your name. Understand?"

"Yes."

"What do you think is the date today?"

I knew it exactly. I had counted the days: thirty-seven days since my arrest, but that was no reason for me to lose my sense of time.

"So you think you know?" he laughed sarcastically. "One more thing, at night you can only pull up your blanket to your shoulders. Your hands have to be above it. We don't want you to choke yourself."

He laughed again and kicked open the door.

* * *

Prisoners were admitted to the showerhead one at a time. The cold water refreshed me. Washing belonged among the pleasures of prison life. I finished fast with the tiny piece of laundry-soap. Today,

I was one of the first taken to the bathroom and there was still a dry corner left on the filthy towel for me.

As soon as I stepped into my cell I noted that my lightbulb was replaced with a much dimmer one. There were only fourteen cells in the Veszprem AVH (secret police) Headquarters. Above the door inside each of the cells a 100 Watt bulb glared day and night. Their blinding light penetrated the hallway as well.

Why the change? Why a dimmer light? Were they trying to be helpful, or did they want to punish me? Was this a new way to break me? What was it that they wanted to know? Fantasies of unthinkable possibilities crowded my mind. Time flew while I sat at attention, staring at the new bulb.

After several weeks of feeding on meager prison fare, I had all the right in the world to feel starved. For the past two months we had had a mess-tin filled one quarter with soup and a piece of bread for lunch, the big meal of the day. I could recognize the different noises in the prison, and I always had a sense of what was happening, like blind people do. Long clatter: the guard pulled the bars shut and locked the outside door. Hollow thud: he put the food container down. Rattling of mess-tins and spoons splashing into the liquid: soup time. Then the clacking of boots: the first soup was on its way.

I heard the first window open. Then the second... The third... then the one right beside me. I'm next... But the boots hammered down the hallway, past my cell. The window after mine opened. Then the next... and the one farther away.

He left me out... that s.o.b. forgot me.

The last mess-tin was passed. Embittered silence followed. I heard the noise of paper as the guard turned the pages of his paperback.

I pressed my ear to the door, ashamed that my animal instinct got the best of me. I was waiting like a hungry lion tied to his bars. I did not want to knock: my self-respect proved to be stronger than my hunger.

Another half hour passed. Then the outside bars clinked. Someone came in. I heard whispers, then the clatter of a mess-tim. Finally my window opened and I got my soup and bread. Why was my food late?

In the morning, guards sealed my tiny cellar window; the last link that kept me in touch with the outside world. This small opening let in the sounds of passers-by and let me breathe some city-air. I felt entombed, my new dim light serving as a votive candle. The noises from the floor above intensified. I heard typing, people coming and going, even shreds of talk from the interrogations.

I thought I understood the end of a sentence: " ...his friend at that Italian company."

Good grief! This could only mean one thing: they had discovered my contacts with Miklos. Impossible.

Against the typewriter's monotonous pecking I heard steps, someone closed a window. All afternoon I listened to the sounds from above. I stretched my ears to catch every fragment of noise, then tried to place each sound and give reason to it. The nothingness of my days made the slightest change into an event and triggered my fantasies. I finally understood the terror of being alone for an extended period of time.

One day the guard mentioned that in a nearby cell someone he called "a bastard suspected of spying" went crazy in three months. Well, I had no intention to oblige them. I just wished that the barely visible dim light did not bother me so much. It shone weaker than in the other cells. Why had they exchanged only mine?

* * *

Lunchtime again. I could barely wait. I listened closely because yesterday's incident still angered me. I heard the splashing ladle, then the outside bars clattered. I clearly heard one of the guards whisper to the other: "Wait with his soup. The doctor isn't here yet."

My heart stopped beating. Who was sick among us? They should take him to the doctor, not his soup. Whose soup were they talking about?

The second window opened, then the third and the fourth. I was next. The window stayed shut. The guard avoided me again. Horror creeped over me and held my heart in its iron fist: it was *my* soup that waited for the doctor. That caused the tardiness. Were they poisoning me? Drugging me?

I forced myself to relax: I must not let my fantasies run away with me. I did not feel any trace of poison or sedative in my body. Finally, after an hour of waiting, I received my soup separately — again — separately.

THE GATES OF HELL

Cold, cold, — I shuddered with cold. Outside it must have been a beautiful lukewarm fall; the end of September. Defying the rules, I pulled my blanket over my shoulders.

Again the strong light from the hallway blinded me for an instant as the guard pushed aside the cover of the peep-hole. I wanted to yell at him, to demand an explanation for his staring. Instead, I lay rigid, clinging to the blanket at my neck, feigning sleep. He said nothing, just slid the door shut.

Since early this afternoon a special guard had read his paperback outside my door. Every half hour he looked through the peep-hole. He didn't reprimand me, he didn't ask anything; he watched.

My fantasies and fears ran away with me: I could not force myself to sleep. I wanted to know what the secret police planned to do with me; whether or not they intended to ruin my nerves.

The soup came late every day now. Obviously I was under medical treatment, even though I felt no need for it.

The guard in front of my door flipped the page in his paperback. I wrinkled my forehead as I gazed at the ceiling. I heard the patter of feet again. An interrogation in the middle of the night?

Men talking — I turned away from them. The spy-hole blinked at me again. I threw myself around. The terror of the unknown overwhelmed me. It was almost morning when I finally fell into a deep sleep.

After the guard yelled "reveille", I forced my eyes open. The bars that separated the upstairs from the prison clanked. Footsteps approached my cell. I ran to the door, eager to hear the conversation.

"Nothing special, sergeant," my guard reported. "He tossed and turned all night, but by morning he fell asleep."

* * *

At night the guard took his usual place right by my door. After "taps" he peeked twice through the spy-hole. It made me nervous to think of what he expected.

Upstairs the interrogations started anew. I couldn't understand how I could hear so clearly through the wall and the sealed window.

Well, at least I could catch the words.

"Sit down!" I heard a strict man's voice.

A chair moved. The same voice continued: "I will listen to what you have to say, Mrs. Balazs."

I got goose pimples. Did they move the Balazs's from Budapest to here? Was the whole case to be tried here?

I felt my veins swell as I tried to listen to every sound.

"Have you known that bastard Tottosy for a long time?"

"Yes." That, without a doubt, was the voice of Mrs. Balazs. Broken and old... yet her voice.

"He was your company lawyer?"

"Yes."

"Did you trust him?"

"Totally."

"Did you know that he swindled and robbed you?"

My hands bent into fists. That's how they were trying to pry something out of her, by playing us, their prisoners, against one another.

After a few seconds the interrogator asked: "Do you believe that the bastard was only after your gold?"

"That I do not believe!" I was glad to hear Mrs. Balazs's denial. Even if she was uncertain and shy... she protected me.

"Where did you get the gold?" was the next question.

"We bought it in 1945 when the Soviets occupied our factory..."

"What do you mean by 'occupied'? The Soviet Union did not occupy factories!"

Mrs. Balazs sounded embarrassed: "When they took it. We had to sign a contract. Whatever we received for the factory we put it all into gold... that is I did... I bought it legally."

"Where was your husband then?"

"He was in prison."

"As a war criminal?"

"He was acquitted. The charge was that he delivered goods to the Germans. Not a word of it was true. To the contrary... He refused a very favorable offer. But this does not belong..."

"Continue!" the interrogator commanded.

"At the end of 1944 the Germans offered my husband two million dollars for all our finished goods: excellent pieces of leather. They even promised we would get passports and we could leave the country. My husband refused!"

"So?!"

"He said the country needed the goods and we wanted to die right here."

"And what happened to the merchandise?"

"The Soviet Army took it."

Silence followed. Measured steps thudded on the floor.

"Didn't it occur to you that both of you were arrested one day before your planned escape?" he continued with his questions. "Who do you think reported you?"

Repressed sobbing was the answer.

"Don't cry. Do you believe that it was your friend?"

"I don't..." the broken woman's voice answered.

The stupidity of the question was surpassed only by its planned malice. How could anyone believe I had denounced myself?

Unexpectedly a woman's voice asked: "Should I put on the next record?"

I felt like I was hit by electric current. Record? Were these people upstairs playing records? Was the interrogation of Mrs. Balazs also a record, recorded in Budapest? Why did they replay them here? For whom? I pressed my hands against my thumping brain. Did they invent this game to break me? The voices from the upstairs room, the rattle of papers, the sighs, the knocking of chairs, — were they planned to break me? This was not an amusement park's enchanted castle, but a prison.

"Don't cry Mrs. Balazs!... You are dismissed for today!" I heard her release from upstairs.

Revving engine noises of an arriving truck interrupted the questioning.

"They are here from Budapest!" I heard the guard's voice. Did he say it upstairs, or downstairs in the hallway? I could not differentiate. I saw it with my mind's eye: a truck arriving, crammed with sweating, trembling nervous people — everyone who had been involved with my escape one way or another. I tried to fit together the pieces of the puzzle from the shreds of sounds. If this was not a nightmare, the AVH played incredibly diabolical theatrics to transport them all here from the capital.

Upstairs a distinguished step aroused my attention again.

"Bring in the next one!" said the interrogator. "Sit down, Mrs. Koltai."

If even she was here, the AVH's investigation of my escape must have delved far back into my past.

"Did you hide your lawyer friend's dollars?" was the first question.

"No," the blonde woman replied. I recognized her soft, but determined voice right away.

"What do you mean: 'No'?"

"I mean that they were not his dollars."

"Whose then?"

"The Balazs's."

"Did your husband know about that?"

Hell of a question: if she said "yes", she would mix in her husband. He played first violin at the Opera. He would lose his job. If she said "no",...

"He didn't," the woman answered.

"So?" the interrogator sounded amused. "You kept it a secret from your husband? Were you your lawyer friend's lover?"

"I beg your pardon!"

"Not so fast. Here you cannot feel hurt about anything. If you confess you might make it easier on yourself."

Obviously such a confession would not have helped her situation, but mud-slinging belonged to the "progressive" methods of the secret police.

The woman was not an easy prey: "I deny this statement," she said softly.

"Even if the janitor testified against you?"

"What could he have lied?"

"For one thing that your lawyer friend visited you several times during the day when your husband was rehearsing at the Opera."

"That is true."

"You see!"

"However, that does not mean anything."

"But it does mean something that he slept at your house..."

"That is not true in this sense."

"In what sense is it true then?"

"He once slept at 'our' house."

"And why?"

The woman seemed to hesitate. "He said that everything was prepared for their escape with the Balazs's, and... he was afraid of being caught. He was certain he was wanted throughout the country."

"Did he bring that up as a reason to spend the night with 'you'?"

"That's ridiculous. My husband invited him."

"A woman can always settle that."

"I deny this accusation."

After his sarcastic laughter, I heard the shuffling of papers as if he looked through some files.

"All right, let's shift to the 'illegality' of the Balazs's. You got them fake I.D. cards?" This last question sounded more like a statement. "Answer me!"

"True."

"Your husband didn't know about this either?"

"No."

"How much did you make on them?"

"Two hundred and fifty forints each, my travelling expenses."

"And your lawyer friend?"

"Nothing."

"Liar! You protect him more than you protect yourself."

"That is the truth. The owners of the I.D.'s got fifteen hundred forints and I kept the five hundred. A ridiculous amount... Their lawyer didn't want to accept anything."

"Why?"

"He said that this was not a proper lawyer's fee. The risk is impossible to pay for and the service to a friend has no price."

"Impressive loyalty!" He pressed her further: "So you are unwilling to tell the truth in front of the judge?"

"What truth?"

"That the Balazs's paid more for their I.D.'s than what you paid to the owners for them, that you had kept the five hundred forints with your lawyer friend."

"The way you say it, it is not true. Only I kept the difference..."

"You will not confess against your lawyer friend, even if I prove it to you that you were his lover?"

"Not even then..."

I heard the door squeak. Someone else must have entered.

Again I recognized her voice, that of a blonde, small creature. She came to my office three times. I handled her divorce. She was the fiancée of a friend of mine, whom I asked to recommend me to his Viennese business friends. This interrogation was shorter.

Next came a lawyer from Budapest, godfather of my child. I could just see his tall figure collapse in his chair when, after a few "do you know's" the interrogator screamed at him:

"I arrest you on charges of conspiring against the State!"

I jumped up from my cot, frightened to death.

This was the end.

The escape, the dollars, the fake I.D.'s all faded away. They had the whole case right in front of them.

I bit into my lips. They knew Dr. Janosi, the M.D., they knew his role... they had every thread in their hands. It no longer mattered that Mr. Maros and all the others didn't know Dr. Janosi. It was enough for them to find one friendship connecting certain names. They'd use it to make up any kind of crime syndicate that suited their purposes.

"I don't know him! I've never heard that name!" Mr. Maros's denial sounded loud and clear.

"If we want, we can make you confess anything. You can be put into the electric oven," the interrogator rumbled.

I wondered if the "electric oven" was that small door beside the entrance? On the way back to my cell after one of my interrogations I fell against that locked door. The guard grabbed me away from it. He looked frightened as he said: "Just stay away from that!" It must have been a slip of his tongue. Could they have killed Dr. Janosi there?

As if in answer to my thoughts I heard the interrogator's voice: "We did not kill him!"

After Mr. Maros came the husband of the woman with the divorce case. He could not tell them anything besides the fact that I wanted to leave the country.

"Did you hear the name 'Veresegyhazi'?" they asked him point blank.

That name was my alias in the organization.

They knew EVERYTHING. Everything that was necessary to open for me the gates of hell...

THE TOWN LOUDSPEAKER

September, 1952

It couldn't be anything else. It had to be the town loudspeaker. I heard it before when the after-the-harvest breeze brought the smell of life into the open cellar window of the prison. Now its words popped like orders from the commander of the execution squad.

"We've already disposed of Janosi in the electric oven. We should try that on Palotai, the leader of the conspirators as well... Or should we ask our lawyer-prisoner first? Will he confess? There is no use denying it. We know his alias: 'Veresegyhazi'!... Nice gang!"

I threw off my blanket and ran to the sealed window. This was not my imagination! I heard it from the outside as clear as a bell.

"Hang Palotai!... Hang Veresegyhazi!" the sound blared as it enumerted our secret code-names.

The dawn came with the blue-grayness of tin.

"Hang... Veresegyhazi!" It was screaming my code name again. I wiped the sweat of my brow and rubbed my ears. The loudspeaker was no hallucination. Since when did they awaken the residents of a town so rudely? It never happened before.

"The secret police discovered a widespread conspiracy," the loudspeaker continued without mercy. "The imperialists wanted to enslave the Hungarian people through armed interference. The American Embassy even gave them financial support. Hand Palotai!... Hang Veresegyhazi!"

I huddled closer to the window to be able to hear the shocking news even better.

"The working people demand the immediate execution of the sentence, without appeal to a higher court!"

"That's an impossibility!" I thought. "Did the secret police go mad? The code of criminal procedure does not provide for such abuse."

I didn't even notice as my prison-door opened.

"What are you doing with your ears pressed to the window?" the guard groaned at me.

"I'm listening to the loudspeaker!" I straightened myself to show that I had nothing to fear.

"What?"

"The loudspeaker!"

"What loudspeaker?"

"The town loudspeaker that is blaring the news."

"What are you talking about?"

"You mean you don't hear it, sir?" I asked, stupefied by his arrogant denial.

"What?"

"What it's saying about the conspiracy."

"What?" He looked at me for a long time. "Do you still hear it?"

I turned my ear towards the window. The loudspeaker continued to crackle its demand for our hanging. I heard it distinctly. The guard lied... He took me for a fool.

"You still don't hear it, sir?"

"Not I!" he shook his head and pointed to the hallway, towards the washroom.

I could see the yard from the washroom. Under a tiny patch of blue sky a minuscule fleece of a cloud hid between the leaves of a chestnut tree, warmed by the sun of the Indian summer. I stopped washing and listened to the loudspeaker. It sounded just as clear as it did in my cell.

"Do you still hear your loudspeaker?" the guard asked curiously.

I nodded.

"You are crazy."

I didn't care what he thought. I looked up to the sky through the small window searching for the sound that always came from above. I heard it much better if I strained to concentrate on it with my head turned upwards and my eyes closed. I staggered back to my cell, but I stayed instinctively by the door. Maybe I'd hear something of what the guards said to each other.

"D'you know what he said?" asked one of them.

"What?"

"He hears the loudspeaker."

"Already?"

Their pretending did not disturb me. I limped towards the window, hoping even the loudspeaker would get tired of the same old text. The town must have had enough of these alarming rumors.

Indeed the text changed: "Palotai's sentence has to be retried by the Supreme Court because of his international connections. However, Veresegyhazi's sentence will be carried out without appeal."

My God, they want to hang me — come what may.

A weakness, characteristic of the feeling before vomiting, welled up in me. Fear of death waved through my stomach like a gush of internal bleeding. I touched my head to the cool, whitewashed wall.

Let the loudspeaker revolt me! I'll be ready for everything — I thought. Let them yell our code-names! I'll show them!

I heard someone move upstairs, in the interrogating room.

"Put on the other record," a strict male voice demanded.

"Yes, sir," answered a woman.

Records again? What is this cruel game?

"Play Veresegyhazi's name again!" the director of this comedy commanded.

"What are you listening for? The loudspeaker again?" the soup-bearing guard asked mockingly.

"Yes!"

"And what is your conclusion about it?"

"Even if a man was insignificant during his lifetime, he can become great in his death."

"Jackass!" He said, slamming the spy-hole.

I barely heard him. What mattered was what happened upstairs. I slowly paced the tiny cell.

"Say it!" I heard the strict male voice again. "The agents of the imperialist forces want to meddle in Hungary's internal affairs."

The loudspeaker immediately screamed the words. Then it demanded I be locked in with Palotai... What? They never locked friends together! Suddenly I realized the possibilities: we could talk. Not out loud, of course, obviously they would listen to every word, the cell must be bugged. Maybe by sign-language or a message on the wall.

Just so...

My hand started to draw letters mechanically.

"Don't say anything about the Americans... Nothing!"

"Look at him!" the loudspeaker yelled. "He is preparing for the talk with Palotai. He is writing his message on the wall... The poor guy, how stupid of him!"

Damn them! How did they know what I was doing? How did they know I was writing on the wall? Was it all in my mind?

My legs couldn't hold me up any longer. I collapsed onto the cot. The guards — they didn't hear the loudspeaker that rang in my ears... or did they? They wanted me to believe that nothing was happening outside, that the interrogations upstairs, the man's voice were all figments of my imagination. I knew that, didn't I? Yes... that's why they dimmed my light and locked my cellar window.

The loudspeaker enticed the population to wilder and wilder things: to capture my friends. My wife and children should be thrown into Lake Balaton and drowned. I should be hanged by my feet. Crazy talk!

"And the lawyer, Maros," it said. He didn't have anything to do with the conspiracy, I thought. They can draw him into this only on the basis of the escape story and that damn hard currency business. "They wanted to make him Secretary of Education." What kind of a madness was that?

I reassured myself by remembering good old Bela, telling me how the secret police linked true events with lies. I saw all the details — I remembered it so well — the last time I met him. His cigarette left trails of smoke as his hands moved. "The AVH," he said, spitting their name, "if they need a trial — they make it up — the witnesses, the evidence, bringing in whoever they want, to say what they want them to say. His voice dropped: "A warning to you — Moscow's sent them blueprints to conjure up another conspiracy trial." He was drunk so I laughed at him for I still believed in the basic justice of the law.

Now I was experiencing a procedure for manufacturing cases, a new method of compiling evidence.

The loudspeaker blared at me cutting my thoughts to pieces.

"Call Dr. Janosi!" it yelled, adding in a sarcastic tone: "Of course, poor Janosi can not be interrogated any more. He died during the night under torture."

They felt so immune. Could they publicly torture?

But no, the loudspeaker retreated: "He hasn't died! The secret police have no torture chambers... He is only seriously ill. They took him to the hospital. They took him to the hospital! They took him to the hospital!"

In my mind, I saw the mass of people in the streets; excited, sad people, listening to this dreadful instigation. The noises from outside sounded like the preparation of an enormous trial. Sentencing was to be done by the people in a completely new and different way.

"Hang Veresegyhazi! But first interrogate him!" the loudspeaker crackled.

Why did it keep saying that — while in here nothing was happening to me?

Dead silence surrounded me. Even the dripping water in the washroom could be heard through the deaf numbness. Yet, not even the water, swishing and rushing down the plumbing, drowned out the tiny scraping sound of the peephole as the guard moved its cover.

There was no interrogation, no inspection of my cell, no reprimands from my keepers; none whatsoever. The guard did not even stop me from approaching the cellar window. I stood there eagerly pressing my ear to the small dirty patch of glass, striving to hear what the loudspeaker said.

It revealed everything: our code-names... our plans abroad... Why didn't they interrogate me? Did they figure out everything by themselves? Weren't they interested in me any more?

Nothing moved in my cellar-world. Only time flew, as if the morning lasted but two hours. The meals... the hunger, lost all meaning. My soup became a mere time-marker.

The changing color of the cellar-window indicated dusk. Its small patch turned black. The sun set behind the hills of Veszprem. I couldn't hear it, but I knew the Church's bells were calling for "Angelus." The end of the bitter day finally came.

"We can no longer interrogate Veresegyhazi... he's dead. He poisoned himself."

I rubbed my forehead against the wall. Good God! They have already announced my death. And why not? Nobody can verify what actually happened to me. Nobody can deny the rumor. However, I still had one card left. I dragged myself to the door:

"Fellow prisoners," I bellowed at the top of my lungs. "The loudspeaker announced I poisoned myself. That is a lie. I am alive and healthy. If I die, then the AVH poisoned me."

I waited for the guards to come and silence me. Nothing — only the quiet of a cemetery. Then I heard whispering from the hallway:

"What did that madman say? Did you hear him? He said he was poisoned..."

The telephone receiver clicked. The guard must have called his commanders asking them what to do.

I probably had only a few minutes to live. The poison must be in me already. I stretched out on my cot. My stomach churned. My heart beat in rhythm with the dripping water. What will I feel when I step over the black threshold of eternity? Only a few more minutes left... or not even that?

I lay with my eyes closed. "Poor guy," the loudspeaker mocked me again, "He thought the secret police would poison someone. He awaits death with his eyes closed. Fool! The AVH does not poison anybody."

I sat up. How could they see through me and in me? Impossible! The truth was... I was alive. The dim light shone right into my eyes.

Suddenly I felt I slandered and misjudged them; I jumped to conclusions. Maybe so. Maybe others are also too fast with their mud-slinging at the AVH. Maybe Bela was wrong.

The loudspeaker reinforced my thoughts: "The secret police does not poison anybody."

The guard handed me a mess-tin. I grabbed it greedily.

"Wait," he said and handed me a small white pill, "Take it!"

What a diabolical trick! First they disperse my doubts — then they poison me! I did not reach for the pill.

"Why don't you take it?" the guard asked. "You don't think I'd poison you, do you?"

Now he was talking about poison too. It didn't matter. If they wanted me to take it they'd mix it in my food. I took the pill and swallowed it before he closed the window.

"Are you happy now, sarge?"

The spy-hole was not even fully shut when the loudspeaker started in again.

* * *

Hammering woke me. "Scaffolds," the loudspeaker explained, "for the hanging."

"They are making the gallows for you!" The lance sergeant leaned against the wall watching me wash.

"I know," I replied.

"How can you be so relaxed about it?"

"If I die for a good cause, I can't act like a coward."

"Do you know why you are going to die?"

"For the freedom of others."

"Stupid fool! You think others are going to be free because the executioner is going to wring your neck?"

I didn't answer.

"Have you seen Bogar, the executioner, at work yet?"

"Not yet."

"Aren't you afraid of him?"

"I am. But, if it's God's will..."

"What 'God's will'?" he grunted, pushing me towards my cell, "it will be the Criminal Council's will, not God's. It's only difficult 'til Bogar cracks your neckbone. Then you'll lose your consciousness. You won't even feel it when he puts the noose around your neck."

The hammering sent chills up and down my spine. The loudspeaker gave me another shock. It announced the death of my mother: she had died of a heart attack grieving for me.

I broke out in dry sobs as I threw myself onto the cot.

What's the matter with you?" the sergeant asked as he saw my tears.

"My mother died!" I answered.

"When did she die?"

"The loudspeaker just said so."

"The loudspeaker?"

"Yes, the town loudspeaker."

"Can you hear that here?"

"Yes."

"You're joshing." He said this in earnest, yet I was certain he was pretending on orders of higher authorities. Only the lance sergeant was honest because he admitted they were preparing the gallows.

"I've heard it with my own ears!" I said.

"Don't try to kid me!"

He left. Why did he deny it? His disbelief must have been part of the procedure of breaking my resistance. I knew the loudspeaker was real — I heard it with my own ears. Yet they pretended not to hear it.

"Poor man! He thinks his mother died. He even told it to the guard. It's not true. Not true!" The denial came from the outside.

I punched my fist into the cot. Some kind of evil was mocking me.

The sounds of the interrogations upstairs filtered down, against the blaring of the loudspeaker; I could hear them simultaneously. The strict male voice dictated to a woman. He listed charges they gathered against me, about connections abroad, about thousands of dollars. The loudspeaker tried to persuade me that the secret police already knew everything. They only wanted to find out how much I would admit on my own accord.

I shook my head. You can wait for that 'til hell freezes over. I won't confess anything. I will say nothing.

"If they already know, they don't need my confession," I reasoned, "If they don't, why would I be crazy enough to tell them?" The loudspeaker's blaring: "Cardinal Mindszenty has also confessed everything!" could not persuade me.

I knew, as long as I was able to command my thoughts, I would not tell them anything, I would remain silent, even if I had proof of them already knowing everything.

I decided I would ignore the threats of the loudspeaker. I wouldn't care that it shouted lies into the world about me forging my degree, robbing my clients. Lies! I wanted to scream in anger, but I refused to make a fool of myself. Every one of my words was reported to the director of this diabolical comedy.

I kept my thoughts to myself. I knew the ways of the secret police; first they set out to prove the moral unworthiness of their victim, to ruin the accused as a human being. The objective charge was never enough. Why shouldn't they treat me the same way as they had treated countless others? They knew people didn't regard political offenses as crimes; they needed to imprint the scarlet letter of moral incrimination on their political opponents in order to rouse public opinion.

I was not surprised by their lies, but they irked me.

At afternoon "toilet" time, a roughly dressed civilian in a cap, normally worn by workers, stood in the hallway. His metal teeth gleamed as he whispered something to the lance sergeant. Instinctively, I paused in front of them:

"Sergeant, whatever that loudspeaker says is a dirty lie," I declared in a sturdy tone.

"What?... How?"

"Yes. Stop pretending you don't know that the loudspeaker lies. Maybe I'll never be able to speak my defense to anybody, but..."

"What are you talking about?"

"To protect the good name of my children, I have to tell you, whatever the loudspeaker blares is all lies."

"Nonsense! Get back to your cell!"

He was not rude, he was almost sympathetic, simply impatient to get me back to my cell.

I spoke my piece; to be able to defend myself, even if only to the sergeant, gave me some peace of mind. I knew there was little likelihood for this sergeant to let the world know about my last words, but others might have heard. They might get a chance. I knew that Mr. Maros, the lawyer, and Mr. "R" were all in this same prison. They could bear witness to the world when they got out, very probably sooner than I would. It no longer mattered what the loudspeaker was saying.

It must have been night when I heard them talking in front of my door. I did not catch the words, but I was convinced they were disparaging me. I knocked on the door.

"Stop abusing me!"

The peephole flew open and the AVH-man's face appeared glowing in the electric light of the hallway:

"Who cares about you here? Shut up or I'll come right in and give you something to worry about!"

Through the hole, I glimpsed the same little man I had seen earlier. He resembled a gray, giant-headed leprechaun. He came to the window and said: "Nobody talks about you here!"

I was still worrried. The loudspeaker ceaselessly demanded I volunteer for an interrogation. No! I won't! Not ever! What for? How could I even start a new "confession"? I wasn't about to describe again, for the hundredth time, the story of my intended escape.

I firmly believed in everyone's right to leave the land where he felt himself a prisoner. Yet, slowly I started to doubt my need to escape. There had to be another way to save the old Balazs's and my own family. I didn't necessarily have to leave my country... Did I even have the right to do so? After all, it *was* my country. Only the guilty flee! Was I without a fault?

In my personal philosophy, the first judge of any case was the lawyer himself, the first judge of the accusations — oneself. Where did rights begin and morals end? I had to face myself, examine my conscience. This was not self-accusation, but self-judgement.

The loudspeaker only threatened because it searched for the truth. I guessed the AVH conjured up all the lies and threats for one reason only: to make me confess the truth. But — I wouldn't! Not to them!

The thought hit me like an electric shock. It made me jump: would the detested AVH also have the right to know the whole truth? Yet, a weak inner voice prompted me to probe deeper into my conscience.

Another voice attracted my attention. It sounded like water rushing through pipes trying to convey a confidential message. I strained to understand the words. The message repeated ever stronger that something had happened to my friend, Miklos.

"It was too late," the voice moaned. "He could not be saved."

"Too late for what?" I grabbed at the air trying to catch the fragments of voice in my fist.

"He could not be saved," the voice repeated. "He wanted to speak the truth, but they killed him."

"They killed him?... Who, how?"

"While shaving."

Suddenly the guard tore my door open.

Now they are going to kill me!

While the guard fumbled around with the lock he said to the other one: "I hope we can get this crazy one shaved. He's likely to cut his own neck!"

So that was it! If I moved my head they could claim I ran into the knife. Two AVH men without stripes waited for me in the hallway. Their blank eyes bored into me. The voice whispered: "This is what they did to Miklos." The loudspeaker followed me with its threats as I walked quietly to my death. I wanted to plug my ears, let myself go. The guard lathered my face. His knife started to glide across my chin.

"He snatched away his neck!" the loudspeaker screeched. "The guard can slice into him any minute!"

A slashed throat — to die like a chicken. I waited with disgust for the geyser of blood gushing forth from my neck after a swift pull of the blade. I sat still, forcing my body to relax.

"Not now, dear God, not now! Don't let them kill me!"

"There's his body!" said the loudspeaker.

I saw Miklos' body lying in the nearby guard's room.

"Stand up!" the guard scolded me.

I obeyed. I jumped to the door of the guard's room. Another guard lay on the bed with his boots on, snoring. This was not my friend, Miklos.

The warden grabbed my arm: "Get the hell out of there!" he snorted: "Back to your cell!"

"Sorry," I muttered, hurrying back, my head cocked to hear the loudspeaker laugh at me like a hyena: "Ernest, you are incorrigible. You still believe the AVH cuts people's throats, eh?"

Now it's calling me by my first name. What did it want from me? I repeated in my most intellectual tone: "The AVH does not poison, or hang anybody without due sentence, it does not execute people in their cells."

I pondered these apparent facts. Nobody has touched me so far. True, they threatened me, they vigorously demanded the truth, but they had the right to do that. They had the right to defend the social order they believed to be good and just. Why would it be inhuman to use strange ways to uncover the truth? The guard could have called the loudspeaker system by phone and reported what I was doing and saying. They had the right. The whole town probably did not have access to what the loudspeaker was saying. I decided this comedy was produced with only me in mind. There could have been a record player right in front of my door. The system's sole purpose was to break me and make me understand: they already knew everything. My importance impressed me.

Yet, I had my doubts: what if all this theory turned out to be a mere figment of my imagination? My thoughts whirled, the loudspeaker alternately encouraging and contradicting me.

"Poor guy," it said, "he thinks we don't know a thing. Ernest, how do we know your alias, Veresegyhazi? Where did we get the idea you were supposed to report in Vienna?"

I clasped my hands on my ears. The words split my brain: "Damn you! You're right! You do know everything."

What else did they want from me?

"You will come, voluntarily, to tell us all."

I shook my head to get rid of an invisible monster. If I closed my eyes I had to deal only with the loudspeaker.

Did I talk to myself? Or was it the town loudspeaker that echoed my thoughts?

If these were the results of the investigations — I had to confess. But I would not let them add a sound to the bare truth. No matter what kind of showcase trials they'd stage, how much they'd threaten me!

In this moment, slowly, haltingly, I started talking, rewording every sentence as I went along, spilling the deepest secret of my heart: I revealed the conspiracy.

In fact it was nothing, it was an act only irrational law would call "conspiracy". We thought and talked of organizing a new political party, other than the ruling Communist party. A few of my friends would gather, trying to work out possibilities for a non-violent peaceful change.

In my rambling, I no longer searched for the ratio of law and power, the bitter rights of a man that got lost in the legal shuffle. This was not self-judgement, or a confession against myself. It was an arithmetic enumeration of colorless, soulless facts marching like lead soldiers in a child's sandbox. I must have sounded like a grocery clerk adding up the bill, murmuring numbers to himself.

"A delegation of the United Nations is coming to Hungary, an international committee will lead the interrogations," the loudspeaker announced.

I sat up with a start. I wanted to shout as joy filled my heart. Finally! Would the AVH dare to stand in front of world scrutiny without censorship?

It didn't matter what the costs would be. For once I could state the truth: not mere facts, but also the moral background, the cause of the facts.

You can shout yourself hoarse, loudspeaker, if we can just get the message of truth across, we will shout to your face: we had the right to organize, the right to gather in the name of morality against lawlessness and terror.

The next communication put an end to my joy: "The People's Republic will not allow the United Nations' committee to enter the country."

I rubbed my ears as hope repeatedly followed despair. In my hopes, I envisioned the questioning at the public prosecutor's office. There I would demand a lawyer, paper and pencil, the right to correspond and newspapers.

If I could just hold out, control my mind until then.

"Taps!" came the gruff voice of the guard.

The yelling hurt my ears. Don't these people care about anything? About the U.N.? The public prosecutor? The showcase trial? The international trial?

I felt rejuvenated as I kneaded my slacks into a pillow and tucked them under my head. I pulled the blanket over me. I was content. The loudspeaker announced it ever more reassuringly: soon the U.N. Committee will be in Budapest.

I heard clutter and talk in front of my door. Two pairs of boots clicked. The changing of the guards. I listened.

"Was he restless?" a voice asked.

"The devil knows," answered another. "Today he didn't shout."

"They've arrived from Budapest!"

Who arrived from Budapest? My excitement returned. The loudspeaker said the U.N. Committee had already landed at Veszprem airport, the town of my prison. I tried to guess whether the committee from Budapest had come to stop them.

This question was more important to me now than the repeated menaces of the loudspeaker. After all, its threats did not cease, yet, no one had hurt me so far.

The silence yawned, occasionally the iron gate down the hall clinked, the spirit-like guard peeked in through the spy-hole. Slowly I took this unusual attention for granted.

I concentrated on the hope that the U.N. Committee would come. I hoped the AVH would not make me an easily hypnotizable helpless puppet before the Committee arrived. I thought of poor "so and so", during the first showcase trial in 1947. He stood mesmerized, begging to be punished for his crimes, confessing to anything they asked.[1]

In legal circles, I heard rumors of a certain poison capable of putting people in such states.

In my half-dream, I recalled a blonde, freckled woman uttering something to me about poisons she had to manufacture...

She worked in a chemistry lab. She could not tolerate her husband's jealousy and they decided on a divorce. I prepared everything for their divorce-agreement, but she did not come any more. In a few months I met her on the streetcar. I barely recognized her. Her blonde crown of hair was scattered, her freckles seemed to have grown in her pale face. At first she did not want to recognize me. She was embarrassed as she said she had to change workplaces.

"I can't stand it much longer," she whispered. "We manufacture terrible poisons, people can be ruined by them, their willpower taken away."

She looked around, terrified that someone might have overheard her...

Two weeks later her husband phoned that he no longer needed a divorce. His wife had committed suicide.

---

[1] The showcase trial of the "Magyar Kozosseg" (Hungarian Community) took place in 1947.

THE VOICE

October, 1952

The style of the loudspeaker gradually changed. Its hostile, stubborn threats continued unaltered, but the text took a form of dialogue between the two of us. Our incomprehensible discussion seemed to take place on the wavelengths of the town's radio newscasts.

I had no time to wonder at this because the merciless voice crackled on: "You thought the U.N. Committee would come, eh? Ernest, how can a lawyer be this gullible? What does the U.N. have to do with an investigation?" The strangest thing was, the voice called me by my first name and chatted informally, as if on a picnic.

"The West does not make sacrifices for anybody," the voice boasted. "Only the Soviet power defends those true to its ideals."

These words crushed my hopes. As if understanding my silent outburst it cried a few words of consolation into the quiet: "Don't be afraid... justice must be victorious." My own thoughts. It repeated the words twice, three times.

What the hell... The damn loudspeaker knew my thoughts.

A door slammed in the room above me. I heard someone's heavy booted steps back and forth across the ceiling. I listened.

"So, what's going on with him?" he asked.

A woman's voice answered, but I couldn't understand. My heart beat in my throat.

"We'll see how strong-willed he is. We'll have to break him," the voice continued, "no matter how much he resists."

They wanted to hypnotize me? Through the walls?

My nerves tensed. I will fight it. I won't let them tear my soul from my body.

Dimly I tried to recall how to fight hypnosis. I had to concentrate on something concrete. I desperately needed an object; the bare walls did not offer much help.

Yes... there, those two big watermarks on the wall beside my bed — they would qualify. One looked like a greyhound, ready to jump, another resembled a little bird with a broken wing. I concentrated on these two with all my might.

Jumping hound, bird with a broken wing!

I struggled to repeat their names. I held my ears shut, my eyes away from the ceiling.

I shuddered from the thought of his eyes penetrating the walls from above.

My eyes searched the cellar window. I didn't know what time of day it was, but I got a glimpse of the sun through the window, barely the size of my palm.

The man's voice from above asked: "Well, is the struggle hard?" His voice held no sarcasm, it sounded rather irate.

The woman reinforced him: "No, it won't work this way."

I felt relieved, I gazed gratefully at the watermark, at the jumping hound and the bird with the broken wing. My defense proved successful. My mind still belonged to me.

My mouth caressed the words to thank my helpmates:... jumping greyhound... bird with the broken wing... jumping hound...

"I can't do it... I can't...," the man's voice sounded angry.

Suddenly everything changed. Maybe I became unfaithful to the two watermarks, maybe my willpower could no longer stand the tenseness... Primate Mindszenty's wide-open, dark-circled, glazed, staring eyes appeared on the white wall, beside my watermarks. He looked into nothingness dazedly, with a glassy stare. I saw his eyes — only his eyes!

I tried to look farther up, to the line of light drawn by the sunshine, but the Primate's eye followed. The eyes grew into a five foot mask drawn with light. I couldn't take my eyes off it. I followed his gaze.

"Now... We got him!" said a voice from above.

I did not protest. I was no longer afraid of being hypnotized. I forgot my watermark helpmates, I relaxed and waited.

"Do not be afraid". It was the Voice: no longer a loudspeaker, but a clear, human voice. It wasn't the strict man's voice from above, but a new, trust-inspiring, friendly Voice:

"Have no fear... follow my command... I can save you!"

Encouragement and the hope for escape was just what I needed.

"Get up!"

I found it natural to obey.

"We'll shake hands," It continued. "Close your eyes!"

I closed them.

"Go towards the door," It instructed me. "Be brave. Go, don't be afraid. I'll follow your every move."

I followed the instructions of the Voice faithfully. I didn't open my eyes, but suddenly I knew I had to be near the door.

"Now... Reach out your right hand and I'll shake it... We are shaking hands... Can you feel it?"

I felt something ticklish on the back of my hand. I trusted blindly the Voice's promise. Despite the order I opened my eyes.

The food-window banged open. A surprised pair of eyes gazed at me. I had never seen this face before. The stranger, a good looking young man in silver-colored overalls, waved his hand in front of my eyes.

I understood: he was checking my reflexes. He didn't say a word, slammed the window shut. The knocking of his boots resounded down the hallway. Was he the Voice from above? Did he order me to the door?

For a few seconds I stood by the door not knowing what to do. Then I heard the Voice again:

"You don't think that I and that young man are one and the same? You guessed right, he is a medical doctor, but he is not our friend. Only we two are true friends. I held your hand. I'll never let go of it any more. I'll guide you as long as you'll need me... Sit down."

I staggered back to my wooden cot. It asked... I answered. It comforted me. Gave me hope. It proved it saw everything that was happening to me. I had no doubts. Through our throughts we talked with one another across the ether.

An extraordinary machine was doing an experiment on me, I reasoned. Within its range, my thoughts could get into contact with the thoughts of the Machine's operator. The Machine saw everything happening around me and read my thoughts. Our dialogue was an exchange of thoughts between two individuals: the operator of the Machine and myself.

The Voice, the operator of the Machine, stood beside this extraordinary invention. I didn't understand how the Machine worked. Though it seemed too fantastic to be true, the only thing that mattered was that the Machine was on my side. Naturally I wanted to know how it worked, but it gave elusive answers to my questions, repeating: "Some day you will know it all... you will know the whole truth."

Technical problems did not hinder our dialogue. New questions kept coming up, I had to answer them all.

The Voice triggered my stream of thoughts by asking, "What do you think?" If I thought "Machine", It immediately answered: "Yes! The Machine! And what about the Machine — would you like to know?"

I believed it could x-ray my soul as well as my body. It had the power to transcend walls and, like an x-ray machine, it could penetrate all the secrets of the human being.

"I'll show you our power," said the Voice. "I'll make you into a living dead. Lie down!"

I stretched out on the cot and waited tensely.

"You will die!" It said. "Do you feel a maiming ray strike your body? Do you feel the slight pain around your belly?"

A small cramp pulled at my stomach. I hardly dared to breathe. The Voice repeated softer and softer: "You will die, but I'll raise you up."

I waited. My brain hammered, circles danced in front of my closed eyes.

"Get up! You fool!" I tried to focus my eyes on the dirty blanket, to make my stubborn limbs move. "Do you believe a human being is able to raise the dead?"

"No... no," I answered in great embarassment.

"See? I am testing you," it went on kindly. "If something will rise in us, what do you think it would be?"

"Conscience," I muttered.

The Voice said dreadful things this afternoon. It assured me that Its death-ray, a special concentrated x-ray, was able to kill a living human cell. The whole thing seemed like a Jules Verne fantasy. The sterile whitewashed walls had no answers to my questions: What power owned this Machine? Where was It located? Right above me, or hundreds of miles away? Was a special team in charge of me? Why did they keep It secret from the world? Where did they service the Machine? Who was my friendly Voice promising help and escape?

My questions besieged Heaven and the Machine. Did the Machine know all my thoughts, and choose to answer only some, a few? Or did some stay within me — unable to cross the ether.

I knew one thing: the Voice was searching for the truth. Precisely, It wanted to know the deepest secrets of my soul. During my usual evening walks, It watched me with cool detachment. I paced the stone tiles of the cell, debating with myself. It praised me for being able to forgive. "Forgiveness gives great strength!"

It told me of a special team in service of the Machine analyzing my thoughts. They saw I tried to hide my "great case", compared to which attempted border crossing was a petty offence. All my inner weaknesses became known to them, my good will as well as my lies. Even my inner struggles were recorded on their sound system.

A new miracle of modern technology, thoughts recorded on a record, unfolded before my eyes. Everything in me said it was impossible, yet, I believed it because the Voice said so; I heard it with my own two ears. It even offered to send the records down to me to prove their existence. I protested:

"I believe you have the Machine! I hear the Voice!"

The contradiction confused me: on one hand It wanted to send me the proof, the "thought-records", through the AVH; on the other, It claimed that the Machine had nothing to do with the AVH.

"Time will come when you will know what the truth is," It kept reassuring me.

Nothing in me could condemn the AVH for trying to find the truth with the help of a new invention. Who could be denied the right to invent a new diving-bell with which to conquer the depths of the ocean hidden in the human soul?

When the Voice spoke of soul, God, and justice, I knew It must have broken away from Lenin's theories. It was impossible for the Voice to be Communist. It even reminded me to deeply immerse myself in my prayers. It encouraged me to kneel while I prayed. It was not my custom to do this, but here — I did it to spite my jailers. I showed them I dared to confess my only inner refuge.

"Don't just rattle off your prayers!" the Voice reminded me. "You know that one sentence uttered with feeling is worth more than a prayer-mill's semi-annual output. Now, do you believe that I am on your side?"

"I believe you," I said, giving my hundredth declaration of trust.

We continued our adventures midst the blunders of my childhood, the years before the war. It saw behind my pretexts, my shady explanations, It sorted out the truth from between my lies.

"How do you know all this?" I blurted out.

"You will see!"

"Do you see into my subconscious?" I stubbornly questioned.

"Of course, it is your subconscious that shows me if you lie. How do you think this method works?"

"Simple," I answered with confidence, "if my subconscious does not agree with my conscious I obviously lie."

"Excellent!"

I became completely numb to the outside world. The Voice flowed, waved, droned all around me. The Voice knew, but did not pry into my best hidden secret: the Case.

I already knew the Voice could not be part of the AVH. It told me over and over, "I have nothing to do with the AVH; I belong elsewhere." It encouraged me, saying It wanted to save me. There was only one condition: I had to tell the truth, the whole truth and nothing but the truth. How could I lie when I knew the records made by the Machine were able to check my conscious against my subconscious, detecting every lie in the process?

I reached mechanically for my soup-supper when the food-window opened.

"Don't slurp! Guard your identity as a cultured man!" It warned me when I lifted the spoon.

The steam of the soup whetted my forgotten hunger, I immersed the spoon in the mess-tin.

"Wait! Control yourself!"

I only ate from the soup when the Voice allowed it.

"You will leave half. No matter how hungry you are, you will hand it out to the guard!"

It commanded and I obeyed.

After taps, I continued the conversation under my blanket, with my head turned away from the ceiling. The Voice took on a new sound. My mother, my wife, my children talked to me. I heard them clearly; they surrounded me with complete chaos in which there was a vantage point. From that point came the comforting questions and encouragement: "... some day you will know everything!"

Morally, the Voice was much sounder than I. It would not accept any kind of embellishing explanations. It saw through the "yes... but's" I habitually used to cover up my flaws or weaknesses. I felt like going through a friendly confession. Its instructions were almost military in their tight-wordedness. It cleansed me to walk through the labyrinth of my past with a strict person. I asked nothing from It, not even sleep.

"Do you want to sleep?" It asked, understanding my thoughts.

"No... not at all!" I protested, greedy for Its company.

"I warn you. Tell the truth!" It reminded me. "I see that today you don't mind staying with me. Tonight, we can talk longer."

It kept vigil with me all night. I lay there with open eyes. Neither the constantly burning light, nor the guard's routine of opening the spy-hole and staring into my cell, bothered me any longer. The warden looked like he wanted to understand my whispers that sounded like the tiny, ticking noises termites make.

After the fear, the dread, and the hours of threats by the town loudspeaker, I welcomed my new, understanding companion... The Voice.

* * *

In every person there is a Machine: the filter of the conscience-machine, the Voice had said. Every thought originating in our subconscious goes through that filter. If our soul longs to find truth, we are able to check the righteousness of our own thoughts. Our inner conscience-machine will tell us which thought is morally right.

I was still alone... when the Voice got tired from our conversations that lasted for days, I tried working my own conscience-machine.

Sentimental thoughts crowded my mind.

"If all that's good and noble would hold hands... "

I definitely felt the warmth all over my insides.

"... if they would give each other... "

I stopped. The inner approval was missing, which showed that the sentence was wrong. I had to look for a new one.

"... and they opened their hearts to one another..."

Yes, that was good.

The inner warmth flowed over me again.

I stood in the middle of my cell contentedly.

I repeated it all: "If all that's good and noble would join forces and open up their hearts to one another..."

I had to continue my thought-process: "... if they'd make a long link-chain... "

Inner approval followed. I continued...

"... and they'd thread together human hearts,

then peace on earth would be born,

and love would rule victoriously."

I repeated it. I walked back and forth between the door and the cot, savoring the row of grey sentences.

"You see?;; the Voice called to me. "You can already use your conscience-machine. But is love possible without truth?"

"No!"

"There is no love without truth!" It repeated. "You can feel it, can't you, the first step is truth. Always tell the truth. Always... "

MY SUBCONSCIOUS

"Don't be afraid!" The Voice woke me gently. "Get dressed fast. The guard will be here any minute to open your cell. Don't let him be rude to you!"

It talked to me like a brother. It kept vigil with me all night and now It recited the poem I wrote yesterday. It advised me not to put on my jacket.

As the silent, indifferent guard appeared at the door, the Voice guided my steps: cautioning me to take smaller, slower paces. It cared about me even in the bathroom: reminding me to take only one tissue to avoid harassment. It urged me to hurry to avoid scoldings. All I had to do was obey.

"What do you think happened to Janosi?" It asked.

"He's in the hospital!" I answered instantly.

"Do you think so?" It said again: "One day you will know, you will know the truth!"

Its repetitions soothed me. I knew It wanted to condition me: It wanted me to understand all Its thoughts.

"What is human thought?" the Voice inquired.

"Human thought?" I repeated.

"Say it again: 'human thought', what can it be?"

"The human thought," I said mechanically "is born when the subconscious transcends into the conscious."

"Excellent!" The Voice agreed. "What do you think, is this subconscious good or bad?"

"Always good!" I snapped.

As soon as I said it an inside nudge told me I was wrong.

"Is it always bad?" I probed.

"Wait!" the Voice interrupted. "You felt, haven't you, that certain power within you, holding back after your assertion 'always bad'. It stopped you because you were mistaken. Search your soul."

My thoughts flowed freely: "My subconscious... "

Voices, softer than breaths, breezed past my ears and I felt rather than heard the one beaming "good" was definitely more powerful than the one suggesting "bad".

Which one was true?

I waited and watched the double reality of my subconscious. It felt as if my soul became a pool and both hot and cold water ran into it. Who played this self-examination game with me?

"See? You found the solution. Your subconscious can't be entirely good or bad. Your subconscious is your soul."

"My soul?"

"That spiritual something that is not identical with your body. It can inspire you to good as well as bad. All your emotions and thoughts go through a filter."

"Conscience?" I asked.

"Indeed. Your subconscious sends out impulses that filter through your conscience: this is how human thought is born. Thoughts emit waves that can be caught, measured and read. They are different in every person. They also vary according to time and space. Do you know their source? Can you name their destination?"

"The subconscious very probably cannot be regulated," I said tentatively.

"But it can be educated. Its safety valve is the conscience. This valve is responsible for what goes through its filter: water or fire, good or bad. Your analysis has come to an end now."

"My analysis?" I asked, utterly disturbed. "I conducted this analysis?"

"But of course. I only read your thoughts on a scope."

I shuddered at the thought that I myself came to this conclusion and the Voice had only been correcting me. I could no longer distinguish clearly where my own thoughts started and where they ended, where the Voice took over.

I stood in awe of my discovery. I had glimpsed at some of the majestic secrets of Creation: I reached an understanding of how I worked. I became acquainted with my soul as it lived outside of me and was inexpressible in material terms.

Contentment, fulfillment, peace washed through me. This intriguing Machine proved to me the existence of a world, outside of the material one. The miraculous Machine proved the self-sustained existence of the spirit. I contrasted our material world, surrounded by rules and laws, with the freedom of the soul. Our creativity, unbound by any structure, depends on our will. We are free to create or remain idle. The spirit shakes loose the laws of time and space; it can soar tens of thousands of miles in one leap and roam through the past, present and future. Human thought is born every minute in the freedom of the complete absence of law.

People get bogged down with the examination of material because that comes easiest. They test their brain like a machine. They try to find the spirit in the material. They forget its engineer, the one who makes the difference. They forget the machine is worth nothing without its inventor. What would a piano be worth without Mozart or Beethoven's music brought alive by an artist?

No, music is not the violin, or the piano. Music is the harmony of the chords of the subconscious turned into conscious. The musical instrument is only a tool. The brain is only a tool, it is not music. How could one explain Mozart by examining the piano?

I clearly saw the relationship of body and soul, the essence of a perfect human being consisting of law and freedom, formed from the bonds of our material world and the total freedom of our spiritual reality. The whole human being: Mozart and the piano.

They both exist separately: the composer and the instrument. Both the spiritual and the material are needed to produce the magic of Mozart's music. Confident in the truth of my conclusions, I knew the Machine recorded all my thoughts on its invisible tape.

"Aren't you paying attention? You damn fool! Are you completely crazy?"

Fast blows of an angry fist on my door shocked me to my senses. I tore my hands off my eyes and stared at the food-window. My body limped to it like a walking corpse and reached for the bowl.

I greedily bent over the steaming soup.

"You are falling at your food..." the Voice scolded.

"Like an animal?" I rounded out the sentence.

"Are you hungry?"

"Very hungry!"

"Even then, don't be greedy. Prove that your will is stronger than your hunger."

"Should I wait?"

"What do you think?"

I obeyed and put the food down reluctantly. The small portion of flavored water teased my nostrils.

I waited, not thinking of anything. I did not want to seem gullible.

"You are unjust!" the Voice scolded. "Do you get hurt if I show you your own subconscious thoughts?"

"No... no."

"You see! You are afraid that I can read your thoughts even in your dreams. Of course I can. The dream differs from reality only inasmuch as your conscious is not working when you sleep. During that time your conscience does not filter your thoughts, but I see your subconscious even then."

"There must be something left from our conscious when we dream."

"Let's just say I am able to find out anything I want about you."

The edges of my world receded, I was falling into an abyss. Nausea and weakness overwhelmed me. I dreamt this before — falling from a rock, an airplane, a train, a flight of stairs, the fear and terror welled in my throat. The shadow of the gallows covered me... waiting.

My only protection against the myriad of threats was the Voice. I covered my eyes. I wanted to shut out even the tiny, blinking light of the weak lightbulb. I wanted to concentrate all my attention on the Voice.

My soup went untouched.

I AM GUILTY

Middle of October, 1952

It came back as a nightmare. It approached my bed in the guise of a monster that made my limbs numb, and invariably planted a lump in my throat when I was a child. I woke to my guilt and terror.

Was I guilty? I hadn't made an honest effort to understand the new power, the human points of view of the Communist system. There must be idealists among them, those who fight for the good of others, sacrificing themselves in the process. There must be some who are unselfish warriors promoting a better world. I had not looked for the forgivable, the understandable, the eternal human in them. I had turned away from them, looking to change them, escape from them. I condemned them without finding out the reasons for their deeds.

I was pretty miserable myself, weak, even evil. I could forgive myself everything, but not them. I measured justice with an uneven scale. I must look for the TRUTH and speak on the TRUTH.

If everyone told the truth, sin would cease to exist. If everyone kept only this one commandment there would be no more unresolved murder, robbery, and embezzlement — there would be no more war. The leaders of a nation preparing for war could no longer hide their daredevil plans, the murderer and the robber would shout their devious intentions to the world.

This wonderful Machine, through its power to read thoughts, could make it possible. There would be no more lies.

A weak electric shock trembled through my body.

"Are you sure?" the Voice asked pointedly.

"No," I answered, ashamed of my feelings. "I shrink from the idea... "

"Continue!"

"... that this Machine might be in Communist hands."

"See? You are still biased! Do you think that in possession of this Machine, someone might still be serving hate? Could he distort the essence of the Machine?" the Voice asked, then continued: "And what is this essence?"

"Love and justice," I answered.

"So, what is your conclusion?"

"It does not make any difference who owns the Machine," I pronounced the verdict, "whoever he is, he has to serve the truth."

"Relax," the Voice encouraged, "this Machine is not in the hands of wicked people. I told you already: some day you will know everything."

Justice, love, sin! What great words. Where do I stand? Without a doubt I was guilty. I hid the upheavals of my conscience like a liar, trying to explain away my shortcomings, I never looked deep into my soul.

"Search your past," the Voice instructed. "Go through the years of your childhood, as if turning the pages of a family album."

Without prodding I was already digging through my memories. I wanted to face my past mistakes. I enumerated my sins, repeating them like the texts we had to study word-by-word in high school. My faults, no matter how small they were, grew into giants. They had to pass through my moral filter. Whenever I tried to cover up the truth, or at least color it, if I wanted to hide from self-accusation, or self-judgment, the Voice stopped me. I remembered completely forgotten details. I sorted them according to time and counted them. Then I started over... from my very first sin.

The Voice swept me into questioning the tiniest details concerning my 33-year life span, as if my short lifetime constituted an unquenchable source of adventures. I enjoyed the cruel dialogue of being my own judge.

Was I seven... eight... nine years old? I stole a stamp from my friend's album. I wanted his beautiful stamps, I was jealous. He had more of the same stamp while I had none. Once he left the big square album with me. He could not possibly notice. I sneaked out one stamp. This was my first theft.

Later, after I went to confession, I had to return it to him as part of my penance. Now this first theft started to burn and choke me. It did not seem like a small mistake, it was a sin: theft.

"You are making good progress!" the Voice rewarded me.

My inner inquisition did not let me rest. The true inquisitor, the Voice, was on guard.

Suddenly — out of the blue — the conspiracy to create a new political party appeared in my mind. I still couldn't consider it a crime. A weakening, numbing feeling of fear filled me. Why did it suddenly appear on the list of my sins?

Was it sinful?... Why?

I filtered it through my conscience, just like everything else. I could not feel guilt, only a desperate fear of the consequences.

Was fear one of the forms of guilt? Impossible. The source of guilt was completely different from the source of fear. Both lived with me as my constant companions: their symptoms were the same as those of high fever and made me just as weak.

I looked for consolation from the Voice with the desperation of someone lost in the woods. I grabbed at Its instructions with trust.

"Are you afraid?" It asked me mockingly. "Don't be! You must tell the truth!"

"How can I lie when you see everything?"

"You have to tell the truth not only to me, but to everyone."

Why didn't the Machine realize I always told the truth to everyone, ever since It started influencing me? I didn't care if they laughed at me, mocked me, and humbled me. I didn't keep it a secret that I was weak, evil and sinful. Why did the Voice always have to remind me?

I already vowed I would confess the truth to anyone, any time. I made this decision not because I was afraid of being found out, but because confession of my sins alleviated the burden I carried around for years. My confession was no longer an act deserving of merit, it became a spiritual necessity.

I knew I could no longer lie. I was guilty... infinitely guilty! Would I be deserving of the Voice's help, despite my sins? I believed myself to be the most culpable among all the inmates in these underground cells.

THE MADMAN

Middle of October, 1952

My sins stood guard beside my bed, waiting for me to open my eyes. The Voice besieged me with Its questions without interruption. At times It consoled me with the thought... "Maybe they won't hang me, after all."

My knees trembled. I remembered my former courage, how I bragged about going to the gallows with my head held high. Why did I now feel hopelessly weak and broken?

"You are afraid, aren't you?"

I didn't need to answer the Voice's question. I cringed in agony. A tiny sunbeam stole its way through the cellar window. I waited for the Voice to speak again.

"I'll save you!"

I stared at the sunbeam without an answer.

"You know, don't you, you deserve hanging for what you have done? But, I will save you. At least I will try. There is only one way to do it."

"What?"

"If you pretend to be mad."

"Me? A madman?"

"Yes!"

I remembered from my readings how madmen were treated: giant attendants, straitjackets, injections, and electric shock treatments... none of that for me.

"I know you are afraid, but it's the only way. They may beat you to a pulp, you may be tortured, you may have to suffer tremendously; you'll have to play your roll well."

"No... I can't. I won't."

"You have to. That's your only way to escape."

"I don't know how."

"Don't worry. I'll coach you, I'll tell you what to do. I am also a medical doctor."

"Also a medical doctor," the words echoed. What else is It, what other things can this mortal machine do?

"I'll lead you out of here, here is death. You can count only on yourself. No one in the world can help you. Do you understand? You must pretend you are mad."

"How?"

"I'll lead you."

I just shook my head. I felt like a weak, inept coward.

"All right, then," the Voice yelled, "you'll hang!"

My dread of torture fought with my desire to escape.

"You'll do it?"

"I will."

I closed my eyes and saw myself batter the walls of a rubber room, beat at the orderlies in the looney bin, the doctors trying to inject me with their syringes, white-clad employees with the straitjacket.

"Don't be afraid. Even if you have to suffer, you will escape. There is only one condition: you have to follow my orders to the letter."

"I will," I gave in with a sigh.

The Voice did not let me relax.

"Get up this instant. Go to the door, we have no time."

I obeyed.

"Close your eyes and don't open them until I say you can. Tilt your head to the side — like that. Now — it's just right — all right, kick the door!"

I awkwardly kicked it.

"Harder," It ordered.

I tried again.

"Even harder... use your fists too... more... harder... kick and bang your fists against that door."

The cacophony of my banging and kicking sounded like thunder in the deathly quiet of the prison.

"Stop it! It ordered "Stay at the door with your head bent down. Shout, at the top of your lungs: 'I want to talk in the Parliament!' Do you hear me? Go on... "

I yelled. I shouted the political blasphemy. I stood there in front of the food-slot, with my head tilted, my eyes shut. My breath shook with fear.

"Don't move. No matter what happens, even if the guard opens the door, hits you, and beats you."

Its order foretold my immediate future.

The food-window swung open and a billy club came crashing down onto my head.

"Let him beat you." It whispered. "No matter how much your blood pours. Don't move! Even if you lose consciousness."

Blows showered my entire body, hitting my ears, and my nose.

"Don't move! Keep going!"

The warm blood from my nose covered my face.

"Goddamn bastard," hissed the AVH guard, beating me with one arm stuck through the food-slot. "What are you yelling about?"

The blows stopped. The window closed.

"You can open your eyes. Good job," the Voice praised me. "You may sit on the bed."

I wiped my nose with my coat-sleeve. My head still pounded. My nose felt as big as a potato and hurt more than my head, but at least it had stopped bleeding.

"It wasn't so bad," I concluded. "If that would just be the end of it."

"Are you crazy?" laughed the Voice. "You think that's all it takes to make them think you're crazy enough to take you to a comfortable mental hospital, put you in a nice, clean bed? No way. Now they just think: maybe you are mad, maybe you're pretending. They have to prove you are crazy. For that, they'll need a medical doctor. He'll come. Do you remember the young man in the silver overalls?"

"The one who checked my reflexes?" I asked.

"Yes. Maybe he will come.. but, you will see."

Unknown horrors filled me with terror. I knew the Voice was preparing me for things to come.

"The anticipation of fear, a normal reaction," the Voice encouraged me. "But if someone enters... maybe the doctor... Don't be afraid of him!"

I must listen to It. I must obey.

I'd barely digested Its prophesy when the young man entered, this time in a white labcoat, carrying a stethoscope. A guard followed in his footsteps.

"Sit rabbit-style!" the Voice screamed Its order. "Pull your arms up to your shoulders, elbows bent, just like a rabbit. Keep your eyes closed. Don't forget. You are crazy! Do not let them pry your arms open."

I shut my eyes, pulled up my arms like a begging dog. They stood around me. Someone slapped me across the face. The Voice commanded:

"Don't move! No matter what they do. They want to make sure you are crazy."

I opened a slit in my eye. The doctor-lieutenant slapped me again. His slap was not an angry one, it felt rather like part of an examination.

"What's happening with you?" he asked softly.

"Don't answer him!" ordered the Voice. "Stay as you are. Don't let them pry your arms apart!"

Two guards tried to pull at my frozen limbs.

"Don't let them!" the Voice repeated. "You'll see what strength I can lend you. Don't forget, you are crazy!"

The guards did not succeed. I just sat in that ridiculous rabbit position.

"Leave him alone!" the doctor waved them to stop. He pulled up my eyelids, then examined my leg reflexes with his tiny instrument.

The Voice allowed me to open my eyes.

For a few moments the little group watched me without a sound, then the doctor looked at my eyes again.

They left.

"You can relax your arms. You did well," the Voice praised me. "Now you can act normally again."

The Voice comforted me, but It did nothing to disperse my terror.

THE CONFESSION

"Be your normal self, whoever comes in!" I knew something was up. The Voice never erred.

The door opened on cue. Mechanically, I got up to face the "evil" lance sergeant. I did not go all the way back to the wall as I should have, according to the rules. He clicked handcuffs on my wrists.

"We cannot let anyone know about our partnership," the Voice warned, "Keep it a secret!"

Clearly, we could not keep the AVH from implementing their plans, but at least I knew what I was supposed to do.

The blond captain, for the first time in uniform, waited for me at the door of the commander's room. He hadn't summoned me for at least two weeks. He stood surrounded by three officers and all the downstairs guards.

"Well, what's new?" he asked in a friendly tone.

"Don't be afraid of him!" the Voice urged. "He is smiling."

"Well, what's new?" he repeated.

"Now!" the Voice snapped the command. "You have to pretend to be mad again!"

I stood motionless, I didn't dare breathe, but the Voice kept after me: "Now, yell: 'I want to talk in the Parliament!'... I order you!"

I bellowed with all my strength. The captain's face distorted, he jumped in front of me and planted his fist in my stomach. I tumbled to the floor, my handcuffed hands tearing from the lance sergeant's grip.

"Don't be afraid!" the Voice strengthened me. "You are a madman again! Close your eyes, these people are trying you now! Hold on to the threshold, even if they beat you to a bloody pulp. Very good... Don't let them pull you away from that threshold. Hold onto it with all your might. So what if the skin comes off your hands. Hold on!"

Blows from their billy clubs crashed on my head. Three guards tried to pull me off the thick, steel-band-reinforced threshold. I held onto it for dear life.

"Good for you! Don't let them tear you away!" the Voice continued its pep-talk.

Hits and blows showered upon me. They tried to kick me away from the door.

"Hang on! The price is your life!" the Voice reinforced me. I listened only to the Voice. I had to play my role well.

My bloody fingers held onto the threshold, but the three angry AVH men finally managed to pull me away, kicking me down the smooth hardwood floor of the hallway. I silently damned this political luxury. I slid all the way to the steps without stopping on that smooth hardwood. I couldn't hold onto anything.

"Don't let them!" the Voice yelled.

They gave me a big push at the edge of the stairs and I tumbled down, with handcuffed hands, head first. My fall was broken by the turn of the twist in the stairs. At the bottom railing I lost consciousness. In the darkness, the Voice's instructions came extremely softly:

"For God's sake, don't open your eyes! Don't spoil everything. You must be mad!"

A kick, — then clinking of the bars. They must have opened my cell door.

They tore off my clothes.

"More trials," warned the Voice. Its prophesies turned into reality with the accuracy of a fine watch. "If they put you under the shower you must continue to pretend madness."

They lifted me into the air and carried me, naked, down the prison hall to the shower beside the guard's room. Ice-cold water poured over me full blast. I sat on the floor, shivering, my eyes closed.

"Pull yourself into the 'rabbit squat'. You must stay in this position, motionless. Don't shiver!"

The unbearable ice-cold water poured without interruption. I followed the orders of the Voice, sitting, eyes shut, arms pulled into the "rabbit-squat." I could imagine the smirking faces of the AVH men, but I wasn't allowed to open my eyes.

The ice-cold water kept pouring, running into every crevice of my body. I finally dared to open my eye halfways. All my torturers stood in the door of the shower, but they had no smirk on their faces. A figure in a gold striped uniform stood by the captain. I recognized him as the AVH man who slapped me after my first madness scene. He stood there with a stop watch, like the coach at a swim meet.

The Voice yelled at me because It noticed the slit between my eyelids. I needed all my strength to hold out. My body was completely frozen.

Finally the shower stopped.

The guards took me back to my cell and threw me on my cot.

"Great performance," the Voice praised me. "Get dressed."

My clothes were piled beside my cot. I shook as I pulled them on.

The Voice prepared me for the next visit: "When someone comes in now, act normal."

"I can't go on!"

"Is that all you can stand to save your life? You want to give up so soon? They merely want to know if your are really mad or if you are just pretending. If the doctor comes in again... "

The chills ran down my spine, but I did not want to contradict the Voice. It gave me exact medical advice. Even if I had to go through the looney bin to escape, it was still better than being hanged. I had no idea how I would get back into the real world, but I had to trust in the secret power of my partner.

"When the doctor comes in, don't be afraid. He is a well intentioned young man. These people are not evil, they just examine symptoms."

Indeed, a new, uniformed doctor came. He held a huge syringe. Only one AVH policeman showed up behind him. All my life I had an aversion to — no, I hated — injections.

"Lie down," the doctor asked more than ordered.

He pulled up my pant leg and his needle penetrated my thigh. "All right," he comforted me. "It's going to be better now."

I looked at him gratefully without a word.

That doctor either believed I was mad, or he was playacting for the guards. By giving me the injection he obviously wanted to show them I needed medical attention.

"See?" the Voice said as soon as the door closed. "See that you have to follow me? You have to suffer for justice, but justice will win out in the end."

I felt reprimanded by Its encouraging words. Was I unjust when I felt suspicious about the AVH?

They had all the rights in the world to be strict with a prisoner who disturbed the peace and tranquility of their jail. Wouldn't I want to test them, too, if they pretended madness? Maybe they were inhuman, but it seemed possible that madmen were treated like this everywhere. The doctor was good to me. His injection must have been for my own benefit. The Voice proved itself right again. Complete truth included every little detail: whether I considered it a sin, or not, whether I was afraid of it or not.

I understood I had to get rid of my sin as well as my fear.

I still did not consider conspiracy a sin, but I was definitely afraid of it; therefore — I had to get rid of it. That was the first step towards becoming clean, towards truth. The conspiracy constantly haunted me, floating on top of my consciousness. Yet, at the same time it also pressed me down, like an unbearable burden.

The Voice interrupted my quiet contemplation: "Your thoughts are being recorded. The confession of truth proves one is on the right track."

I could not quite grasp why I would have to openly confess

something I did not consider a sin, but I had to bend to the will of the Voice.

People are not your enemies, your enemy is Denial, the spirit of Denial which lives within you and holds you captive. You have to fight this spirit. Everyone instinctively searches for truth. You have to tell the truth always, everywhere.

Did this mean that Denial was my enemy even without the feeling of remorse? Everything I tried to keep secret automatically became a sin?

"You are on the right track," the Voice approved my voluntary soul searching. "Forget for a moment the difference between sin and fright. Think of the fact that lying is a sin in itself. To deny a fact is lying."

"Even if the confession of the fact would cause the end of me?"

"Even then. You have to tell the truth."

The forever haunting picture of the young interrogator appeared in my mind. More than a month ago he referred to Cardinal Mindszenty and said: "The time will come when you will tell us all else you know, voluntarily."

"You do remember, don't you?" the Voice followed my every thought. "What did that interrogator ask you at the time?"

"Whether I had something else to confess."

"And what did you answer?"

"No."

"Did you lie?"

"I lied."

"Is lying a sin?"

"It's a sin."

"Were you guilty of denying your terror, your organizing?"

"I was guilty."

"Do you promise to tell the whole truth now?"

"I do."

"Are you willing to follow this truth? Are you ready to retract this guilty lie and confess the truth?"

"I am willing."

"Truth is the greatest value," the Voice repeated. "Tell the truth, no matter who asks you."

The clinking of the key drowned out the repeated warnings of the Voice. A good-looking young man in civilian clothes entered my cell.

"Good day, Mr. Attorney, do you have something to say to me? I would be pleased to listen..."

"Here's your chance. Tell him you want to confess," the Voice prodded.

"I want to confess, Lieutenant," I said. I don't know how I knew his rank. I felt compelled to tell him whatever floated onto the top of my terror-stricken consciousness. I had to prove to him: I valued truth even more than my own life.

I followed the civilian to the first floor. No guards anywhere, the room of the commander stood empty.

"Sit down," he said, pointing to a chair where I often sat during interrogations, in front of the AVH commander.

"Tell him you are not worthy of sitting," the Voice commandeered.

I said so, choking on my tears. "Lieutenant," I continued as if I were certain of his rank, "I am willing to sign. I will not ask for mercy."

"Forget it. We have not reached that point yet. Just tell me what lies on your conscience."

The black-haired typist was already in the room. I used to call her "ratty Communist witch" in my thoughts. Now I felt I should apologize.

"Well, Mr. Attorney?" prodded the civilian.

I avoided looking at him. Instead, I looked at the ceiling. I expected the Voice's instructions from there.

"Tell the truth," It urged me. "Just like you told me hundreds of times, rehearsing. Don't find excuses!"

"In 1947 I met a doctor who had the same political convictions I had," I started.

Words poured forth, sentences I rehearsed in my cell, reciting them to the Voice. I hid nothing. My story, my confession, was short but true. The way I got involved with the conspiracy, my preparation for escape to the West developed during the course of the story. I stopped now and then, waiting for the Voice's approval.

The typewriter clicked, my interrogator listened without interrupting me. He meticulously repeated everything that I had said. At the end he asked: "Do you want to read it?"

"No! I heard your dictation."

"Sign it."

My hand shook as I took his fountain pen.

He escorted me down to the cell. No guard was in sight. The whole scene seemed to have been prepared for our conversation. As we entered the cell I felt some mysterious inner power force words on my lips. Jibberish bubbled out of my mouth about "goodness," "truth," and "human love."

The civilian listened to me, then held out his hand.

"Let's shake hands on it: from now on you will always tell the truth," were his parting words.

It hurt me that he, too, should remind me to tell the truth.

I confessed the facts because I was ordered to do so. It was not a guilty self-confession, but the proof that I dared to tell the truth about everything.

I stood dazed in the middle of the cell.

I felt dizzy, painful wounds on my hands... I remembered pretending to be mad... the understanding looks... the injection... the doctor... the friendly prodding... and the confession. THE CONFESSION — told exactly as it happened. But for that I can hang! Jesus... hang. Exactly as the town loudspeaker of Veszprem had announced it. I pushed my head against the hot stillness, from which no more Voice came.

It disappeared! It no longer called, prodded, approved. Stillness... horrifying, paralyzing quiet surrounded me.

Where is the Voice?

Icy terror crept into my heart. I could not hear anything, no matter how much I twisted my head towards the ceiling. God! Could I have fallen into some despicable trap? Had they persuaded me through hypnosis, poison, or God knows what diabolical procedures to confess?

My thoughts raced around in circles: "Voice! Where are you? What did you do with me? What have I done by following you? I am mad — really mad. I told them everything, baring my own life and those of my friends. I became putty in their hands; a mere puppet."

I fell onto the cot, pulling my hair like someone who lost his mind. My wounded hand dug into the skin on my skull.

Was I actually crazy? Had my pretending led me to this? What did I do? Why did my mind leave me? Why did God leave me?

I jumped to my feet and started to pace up and down my cell. I had time for only three or four turns, wallowing in the murderous twists of self-accusation, when the Voice started talking again. It sounded as clear as a bell: "Did you doubt me? Don't you believe in truth? How many times did I prove my existence to you? How many times did you concede that I led you to truth?"

I grabbed Its invisible, outstretched hand. The resurrected horrors subsided. If the Voice wanted me to hand my head to the executioner, It would also know how to lift it out of the noose.

THE SHADOW OF MY SINS

What kind of person is hiding behind that Voice? Is It an old, bearded scientist, or a middle-aged manager type? I didn't dare ask. If It could read my mind, It did not answer this question. The Voice was silent about Itself.

"We are searching for your sins, not for your good deeds," It reminded me. I finished my meal mechanically, bent my head and dug into my memories.

Why was I suddenly on the Soviet front, in the dreariness of the Second World War? Did It want to get acquainted with that "me", that totally mixed up young man, that was thrown into the war?

A cold snowstorm raged bitterly. We drove across the frozen Dneper. The total whiteness of the landscape stretched into the horizon undisturbed by any sign of life. We searched for a Russian kolhoz where we could rest awhile. Finally we found the tiny houses in the desolate snowfields. We loaded up with some essential food and hurried back to Dnepropetrovsk. We wanted to get there before dark. Constantly twirling light snow covered the roads. We lost our way. Our truck puffed heavily up the mountain. We asked for directions from the first people we met. We had strayed way off course, we were almost behind Soviet lines. As we prepared to start back, an old man in a grey parka yelled after us: "Stop! We have a holiday today. Warm yourself with a little drink. Here!" He stretched his vodka-jug towards us. Suspicion ran through me: what if he poisoned us? Then I looked into his eyes. They radiated such warmth, my fright melted away.

I drank. I never liked vodka, but this time its warmth spread throughout my frozen body. I handed it to my mates in the truck; they too had a slug.

He could have poisoned us, could have sent us the wrong way, but the old man behaved as a brother. And how did I reciprocate? I did not share with them the food rations I managed to save. I asked for something in exchange. I wanted their trinkets. Good-will was not enough for me. I asked for a price even from those who were starving. This was not humane, it was merely legal.

Another memory came haunting: I walked through the market of Dnepropetrovsk, Christmas of 1941. Cruel starvation forced the population to sell their small valuables.

I had one shiny can of food left, a two-pound German military can. I wanted to trade it for a souvenir for my fiance, for my parents. A long-haired old man pulled a small blond child in front of me. I saw the two wandering hopelessly in the 20 below weather. They no longer had anything to exchange. Tears ran down his old face as he muttered "kushat" (eat). He explained as best he could that the child's parents had escaped to the Urals and left him with his grandchild. A dark feeling came over me: what will happen if the war turns on us and these starving people come to our country? The awareness of senseless suffering blew my mind.

I gave them my leftover can of food.

"You are bragging!" the Voice scolded. "Good deeds do not cancel out the bad!"

I wandered out again and again to see the infinite magic of the prairies broken up by machines of war.

We could not see the end of the dusty highways and we were lost from our company. As corporal at the time, I lead several men towards an unknown goal. Broken in spirit as well as in body we reached the next village. We stepped into the first house we found.

Four Germans sat around a table: members of a radio squad. They tended to their duty as if the fate of the Eastern Front depended on them. As faithful servants of "General Duty" they held up that link of the chain which was theirs to hold in this gigantic war machine.

We were tired, dusty, hungry. They shared their simple lunch, politely, humanely. They called it comraderie. We saw it as much more: as brotherly love.

We saw more Germans, links in the same chain of war, driving prisoners from Kiev like a grayly waving herd of rats. If someone stepped out of line, or dared to stretch out his hands for a potato or cucumber, he was shot on the spot. For the sake of "order" this ghostly troop of inhuman people turned into mere animals.

Something went wrong with human nature!

"You have to pretend to be mad again!" said the Voice waking me from my state of reverie.

I did not resist. I followed Its step-by-step commands obediently. I went to the door, closed my eyes and started yelling the text It inspired: "The lance sergeant is a stupid Communist bastard."

The guard tore my window open and screamed at me:

"What are you yelling, you damned fool?"

I bent down my head and answered:

"The lance sergeant is a stupid Communist bastard."

The Voice stayed with me, "Don't worry about it if he brings the billy club. Don't move, no matter what he is doing to you."

The first blow came. "Don't move!" I heard the Voice. Blows showered all over me. Something in me prayed for mercy.

"What are you fretting about?" the Voice reprimanded. "You haven't died yet, have you? Stay quiet."

"Dirty beast," hissed the lance sergeant. He hit me on the head, full blast.

Warmth poured over my face. If this was blood, it meant my torture would not last much longer. The Voice asked me to be a madman only 'til the first blood appeared, He stopped the blows and shut the opening.

The bleeding stopped, the pain subsided, the guard yelled taps. I stretched out on the cot and stared at the ceiling.

"See the Russian villager waiting for her husband?" the Voice said taking me back to my memories. "She will be waiting forever. It took a mere click of the trigger. The Germans had the power and it made them mad. See, how power can make a person mad? That is why you have to become crazy, to be able to get rid of the AVH. You must know, mad people respect only other madmen!"

"Like Rakosi, the leader of the Hungarian Communists?" I interjected involuntarily.

"What do you think, is he a madman?" The Voice retorted.

"He is an evil man."

"Maybe you are wrong. Maybe no one is evil, only circumstances and power make him this way. Do you think the Russian soldier who shot because Stalin ordered him to shoot, or the German one who followed Hitler's orders was evil?"

"None of them was guilty."

"See, sin comes from the outside. One absorbs it like the parched soil absorbs water."

"We drag it around with us."

"It sticks to us like our shadow. Don't stop, continue with your memories about Russia. It will become even clearer to you, how much you have sinned."

I collected things. It started with saving all kinds of paraphernalia with the Soviet red star on it. I pinned them on cardboard, the way collectors display butterflies.

Then came the icon-fever. We went from door to door in search of icons, exchanging all we had, all our hoarded food. Their value or age was not what interested us. We wanted them for some kind of a trophy, after our return home. The Russian population seemed to have lots of icons lying arouing among their secret treasures. Ukrainian peasants kept and hid them despite the religious persecution aimed at the faithful to make them forget their tradition. They gave up their treasures for food. The gold-guilded, ceramic, silver and metal-plated holy pictures emerged from walled up attics, from underground chambers. Their metallic shine blinded me now as I remembered them like exhibits in a Museum of Crime.

"Why did you collect icons?"
"It was a passion."
"Do you feel good about it?"
"No. They were holy pictures. I shouldn't have..."
"What should you have done?"
"Helped the starving without asking for anything in return."
"Can you feel the weight of your sins?"

I sat motionless all day, bitterness flowing through me. The shadow of the small grate above the cell door was projected on the ceiling by the weak lightbulb. I covered my eyes in order to be able to concentrate on the pictures of my past.

"Don't cover your eyes! Look at the lightgrate," the Voice warned me. "It is an omen."

A wave of fear swept over my heart. My eyes were glued to the grate created by the light and shadow.

"It's moving."

The light-shadow slowly started waving, then turning in a uniform circular movement.

"See?"

Soon a tiny shadow-figure rose from one side of the grate, then it moved to the other, finally it disappeared.

"What was this?"
"Take another look."

The shadow-figure moving out from the bottom of the grate was like an angel with wings spread out. A second shadow rose from beside it, then a third. They rose from the bottom of the grate to its top, only to disappear into nothingness.

"Tiny angel-shadows," I whispered uncertainly.
"Yes, they are. I projected them there. What do you think all of this means?"
"Death!" I moaned.
"You got it."
"Who died?"
"Your father-in-law."
"Poor old man."
"Someone else too."

I watched terrified at the ever increasing number of angel-shadows.

The Voice mercilessly continued: "Your mother!"
"Oh God!" I could not continue.

The angel-shadows disappeared from the grate, the mad carousel slowed down and the lines of one lonely face took shape above the grate: my mother's. The picture was clear, unmistakable.

The apparition disappeared. Tearless weeping choked my throat.

THE ORIENTAL "ME"

When the Voice scared me out of my sleep I forgot the sad news of the previous day as if I'd never heard it.

It swept me into a very different world, into soaring heights. We sped through dangerous curves of twisting serpentines amidst tremendous rocks. I heard only the Voice's stacatto explanations: "That tiny car, right there, at the edge of the cliff. Some day it might carry you. This infinitely remote world you see is closer to truth."

"Where are we? Where are you leading me?"

A soft distant voice, much softer than the usual messages whispered: "... somewhere in Asia, Christians, Jews, Brahmans, Buddhists, Moslims, scientists and psychologists live in a brotherly community. Far from the fights of civilization, power struggle and neon lights, they search for truth on top of the world, in the peace and quiet of the Himalayas. That is where the Machine is situated that works with you. This astrological research station examines the human soul... "

I felt a fervent desire to work among them, anonymously, like a humble ant. The concept — to avoid the dust of everyday and to absorb the pure delights of truth — lured me.

"How would you like to part with people for a long time?" the Voice asked.

"From my family?"

"Completely. Imagine yourself a soulsearcher in the tall mountains, with ultramodern equipment, in celestial peace. There you would be working among the others."

"Is that where the Machine is? Or do you have more than one?"

It did not answer.

The question tortured me: of what possible use could I be if they had the Machine? I wondered if they would send me there in punishment, or if my past had revealed some small merit among my sins which would make me eligible for this exquisite, majestic exile.

Joy, rapture, surprise, hope swirled through my whole being mixed with a desire for the great meeting with oriental lamas, philosophers, scientists, unknown mystics.

Was it day or night? Did my adventure start yesterday or a week ago? Nothing mattered. My environment, food and sleep became irrelevant. Fright and guilt dissolved in my feeling of increasing importance, then it melted into humility.

"Do you believe in God?" the voice tested me.

"Of course I do."

"How do you see Him?"

Blinding rings of light twirled fast in front of my eyes.

"I see him as I see these rings that come from nowhere. A tiny spark bursts forth from an enormous light: this is man! It breaks away from the infinite light and twirls around in darkness until the great light attracts it back onto itself." Enchanted by the spiritual content of our conversation and by the magnificence of the pictures projected, I wondered: was this the work of the Machine?

I saw a tiara-crowned head, one side covered by shade.

"Who do you think that is?"

"The Pope."

Another, yellowish face appeared with high cheekbones and slanted eyes.

"And he?"

"The Dalai Lama?"

Maybe..."

We flew over high mountains. A tiny patch was visible from above the summits devoid of foliage, above the snow-covered giant peaks. Abysses and treeless, bare flatlands varied in the landscape with the impressive mountains. We came closer to the ground.

I remembered a poem I wrote when I was a student, about "Turan":

"Sleep overwhelmed me once as I was reading,
And on a spider's web,
On a thin silken thread
I descended to the depth.
Sandor Csoma fired my imagination,
And I saw his people, like a revelation,
A fabulous nation.
While snow-covered peaks were towering above me,
I saw strange, silent men walking in the valley,
With slanted eyes peering from their yellow faces,
And tiny prayer wheels revolving in their hands.
None of them did I feel brave enough to address.
On the vibrating lute-strings of my heart
Ancient Turan had played a tune that night."[1]

"Go on!" the Voice prodded.

"I can't remember..."

How did I recall this **poem? Dust had collected on it for the past** ten years, among the mementos of my student days. Did some atavistic power throw it on the level of my consciousness?

---

[1] "Turan" the poem translated by Susan Jancso.

A weak breeze whispered in my ear: "You stem from an oriental seed, an Asian root, transplanted into the soil of the West. Your body and soul are like a several thousand year old church which is under continuous restoration. It stays in its age-old form, but only a few tiny pebbles remain of the original structure. The cells of your body change, but something of the Asian seed remains in your genes forever."

Even if at one time the Hungarian people came from Asia, if we were related to the Japanese, the Mongolians, the Chinese... I saw myself as white and European. The sensitive mysticism and savor of the East and the reality and color of the West participated equally in the creation of a Hungarian.

The black, almost almond-shaped eyes of my younger daughter showed a bit of Asian character. I could just see her dark, shining eyes. The more convinced I became that the miraculous truth-seeing Machine had to be in the East, the more the Eastern "seed" grew within me.

The weakened light moved on the dirty ceiling of my cell.

"Are you showing me something?" I asked the Voice.

"Look!"

I opened my eyes and looked at the spinning bars with foreboding.

The pale face of a child appeared. There were two empty holes in place of her eyes. "Oh, my God!" I moaned. "What happened to the child? Why does she look at me with those two holes in place of her eyes?" I groaned and screamed my questions to the Voice. I watched the bars slowly become fuzzy.

"Unfortunately, my friend, your younger daughter's eyes..."

"Did somebody poke them out? Who? How?" the questions crowded around in my brain.[2]

I tore at my hair. I did not even wipe my tears away.

"The Eastern man does not despair," the Voice reprimanded me.

What did I care if I was Eastern, or Western? The suffering parent in me had no race, or place.

Does God want to punish me as He did Job?

"Why did the monks in the Middle Ages whip themselves?" the Voice asked.

"To punish themselves."

"Do you think the Eastern man does not punish himself?"

"He does."

I realized the necessity of self-punishment. I decided: I will make the guard beat me.

At morning wash-time I prepared to put on my dirty, bloody coat, when the Voice commanded: "Don't put it on!"

---

[2] At the same time my younger daughter almost poked out her eyes with a knife and seriously injured herself.

"Why not?"

"The Eastern man does not hurry with dressing. Wait! See, even half-naked you are not freezing. Get used to it!"

The Voice was right. I did not feel the need for a coat. I paced back and forth in my cell and the cold of the prison did not bother me.

After breakfast when the guard came in the Voice dictated: "Now!"

"Mr. Inspector," I started and stepped to the guard.

"What is it?"

"Please, slap me across the face!"

He looked me up and down: "What?"

"Please, give me a slap!"

"Are you crazy?"

"I want to repent!"

He waved his head in disbelief and turned around. He wanted to leave, but I stood right in his path.

"Mr. Inspector, I demand you hit me across the face."

"What? You dare to demand?"

"Yes. If you don't slap me, I'll punch you in the stomach."

He straightened himself, turned and lifted his boorish palm with savage rage. It came down hard onto my cheek.

"If that's all you want, here! Take it!"

I swayed.

"Did you turn into a pendulum?" The Voice held me accountable for my involuntary movement. "The Eastern man does not even budge when they slap him. You must ask for another one."

"Mr. Inspector, that was nothing," I repeated the Voice's words though my face ached and my ears buzzed from the blow. This time when he hit me, I managed to keep my head straight, but I almost lost my balance.

"Ask for another one!" the Voice ordered.

"That wasn't strong enough either!" I egged on the guard.

He hit me full swing. I stood like a tree. He looked at me stupefied and trudged out without a word. I must have passed the test. The Voice reminded me of the oriental scientists in the clear, clean mountains. Unexpectedly it interjected the thought that outside the sun must be shining. Indeed, the usual ray danced on top of the cellar window.

"Look there... that looks like a top hat!"

Above the door, under the constantly burning lightbulb that looked much paler on account of the sunlight, a brown water spot appeared on the wall.

"Watch it!"

My eyes were glued on the form that started to grow and twirl, until it became three dimensional, like a real top hat. It moved out from the wall, then doubled in size. The twirling stopped and it returned to its original form. The rays of sunshine danced again on a mere brown water spot.

"What was that?" the Voice questioned.

As I had no answer, It explained: if someone had the gift to use the power of suggestion, it was possible to increase that through the transference of just the right amount of strength. "Look at that pear-shaped spot!" the Voice concluded.

Obediently I concentrated on altering the water-spot, to make it grow by exercising my will. I managed to make it three dimensional, double it in size, then make it return to its original shape and form.

Was this practice aimed to introduce me into the mysticism of the East? My self-esteem swelled, I thought about my Eastern seed with secret pride.

The Voice interrupted as I ate. "Discipline yourself! Don't eat! You know you must repent."

I put down the spoon without resistance. The Voice finally let me finish, but only half of my soup, after thirty minutes of conversation. Without any apropos the Voice returned to the terrible sight of the night: the poked out eyes of my daughter.

This time it made me doubt: maybe the horror was not true, after all.

But, it almost was.

EXAMINATION OF CONSCIENCE

Around the end of October, 1952

Why did I look for the Machine in the Orient? Why should it be in the monumental mountains of the Far-East? Why am I attracted by the memories of mountainous regions? The Monastery in the mountains of Rila looked just like these at the time of my Bulgarian excursion in 1940.

The top of the Bulgarian world presented a majestic sight. Pilgrims, mainly foreigners, peeked curiously towards the onion-shaped domes from the termite ridden centuries old porch. On the summits of the Rhodope snow remained despite the warm summer. The winds of war left tourism unaffected in these parts. Rila knew centuries of isolation, the monastery among the snow-covered mountains often had to withstand the plundering of the treasure-hungry Turkish fanatics.

"What is the meaning of all this?" asked the Voice.

Another memory floated through my thoughts — again in the mountains. We tried to climb up the Vitosa in pouring rain; much smaller than the Rila, it was in no way suitable for a soul-searching establishment. The Ministry of Foreign Affairs had assigned me to a Bulgarian journalist, some Kraf...

"Krafcsen?" I thought.

"Can't you remember his name? You've forgotten the name of a world-famous author?" the Voice prodded. "Was he really a Bulgarian or maybe a Russian?"

I raked my mind — in vain. Searching for something to jog my memory, I rubbed my eyes. The Voice laughed as it said: "I'll help!"

That instant the name flashed through my mind: "Krafcsenko!" That Machine must have paralyzed my mind earlier. I desperately tried to clear my senses and be in full command.

The Voice mumbled at me: "Someone might be coming." Who? And from where? I didn't know. I only knew I would have an opportunity to ask for punishment again. Whoever came had to be a good man. No evil men walked the face of the earth outside of me.

The door's screeching halted my thoughts; the blond sergeant walked into my cell.

"What does he think about you?" the Voice whispered behind my ear. "He must be sorry for you. See, he is not a bad kid. Maybe he himself doesn't know what the AVH stands for. Have they hurt you so far? **A little pushing, or making you lie down under the shower is nothing. Have they killed you? Have they poisoned you?"**

I had to concede: the Voice was right. Whatever they had done, I deserved. It was just punishment.

The blond guard said nothing, he only looked me up and down; nothing in his attitude betrayed his intentions to hurt or help me.

I heard the Voice again. "Help?... Of course!" I knew what I had to do.

"Sir, slap me across the face, real hard," I begged.

"What?" the sergeant sounded shocked.

"I demand a slap."

I employed yesterday's trick again and promised to punch him in the stomach if he did not comply with my wish.

"You're pulling my leg!" he said in astonishment.

"I'll hit you in the stomach."

"Me?"

I felt sorry for him. It would be mean to slug him just because he was not in the mood to slap me across the face.

"Please, forgive me, Sir."

"Why do you want to be beaten?"

"I want to do penance."

He shook his head. The Voice proved itself right again: he could not be evil.

"Why haven't you eaten your soup?" he asked good naturedly.

"I'm disciplining myself."

"Do you want to see your family again?" he asked, looking back from the door.

His question filled me with hope. He does not find me such a great criminal after all. He is looking out for my health. How had I deserved this?

I found another way to do penance. **I stood at attention on top of my bed, hands by my side. I endured, frozen into position, while the Voice scolded and instructed me.**

It added new crimes to the already unbearable burden my conscience was carrying. New, hitherto unseen evilness came to light. It amazed me I never considered these acts sinful before. I had not even thought of confessing them. The Voice made me realize how much people rationalized when it came to moral values. No lie escaped this strict judge: I had to punish myself.

The evil lance sergeant stood in front of me on his crooked legs, knitted his brows and said: "Well, what's going on, Uncle Ernest?"

What had happened to him? How could he have changed so much? Or was it me who suddenly started to see clearly, to observe people in their own reality, without any of my old prejudices?

I could not feel an ounce of mockery in his tone. Shame crept over me for having called him a dirty Communist. He had the right to beat me, I deserved it. He was not any more or less evil than the rest of them, they had the right to fight for their truth. He looked at me without a word and I looked back at him without fear.

The Voice was right. If I did nothing wrong, no one would hurt me. Punishment was only used to render justice. I simply had not recognized truth among all the deception and lies until now.

Sweat beaded on the lance sergeant's lip as he struck me. I saw the billy club in his hand, I almost asked him to hit me with it. My cowardness, my fear from pain wouldn't let me. I asked only for a slap. I took this much better than the other blows.

More incriminating memories followed:

I saw an autumn afternoon pregnant with rain. The acacia trees of Budapest were bent over, forced by the wind. On the other side of the road an old woman approached, her head bent down like the branches. I recognized her, she was my French teacher who tutored me in the language of Moliere and Voltaire. Her wrinkled black dress bore a huge yellow star. War ruled in our country, my uniform burned my body with shame... She came on the other side of the street. My relief at not being "forced" to notice her was my crime.

Maybe she hadn't noticed me either.

"Oh yes, she had!" the Voice jumped at me. "I am sure she saw you, she knew her pupil who, on account of his uniform, avoided the leprosy of her race. What should you have done?"

"I should have gone to her."

"That's right. You should've. Instead, you were happy to have been born on the 'other side.' Symbolically you threw dirt at her."

"I see it now."

"Now you know what a coward you are."

I became weak from shame, the depressing picture choked me. I wanted to rip myself out of the black-clad old woman's accusing look.

"I was brave, sometimes," I stuttered in defense. "Once I practically defied all powers by going up to a schoolfriend of mine. I had not let my uniform restrain me. He almost dropped his dirty little bag in which he carried all his belongings as an inmate of a forced labor camp when he saw me approach. He pulled his bag in front of the yellow star to cover the ulcer that brought shame not onto its bearer, but unto the system.

The Voice waved away the case. "Don't brag! We are not interested in your good deeds, but in your sins. Would you dare to confess them publicly?"

"Why not?" I burst out in anger. Confession belonged with repentance. Silence.

Peculiar, even in the accusing, great silence I heard a disturbing noise. Tiny, foreign, unintelligible bits of sound surrounded me, populated my silence. A flute-like, slowly fading tone accompanied the words of the Voice, then it turned into a finely buzzing whistle. It sounded as if the network of water-pipes, criss-crossing the entire ceiling of the cellar and the water running from open taps all melted into a curious melody of water music. The melody resembled sad organ music accompanying a church choir. At times it rang out full force, then it died down slowly, only to resume on a new tone in a few seconds. Was it truly the waterpipes that produced this sound, or a record, a choir, or the Machine?

I followed the cacophony in a daze.

Suddenly all became silent. Knocks sounding like waterdrops disturbed the quiet. They horrified me because they talked: "Crook! Scoun-drel!" over and over they articulated. "Crook! Scoun-drel!"

Boots hammered down the hall. They too boomed: "Crook! — Scoun-drel!" They were right, I did not deserve mercy, not even from God.

"Is that the kind of Christian you are?" the Voice inquired. "You remember God when you are in trouble?"

I remembered something else: prayer. I hadn't prayed for weeks, months, who knows how long. I should have said the whole rosary at least twice a day, as I vowed a long time ago. I knelt down in repentence beside my cot, just like I did during the first days of my imprisonment. Then stubborn defiance led me; now I knelt no longer of stubbornness and defiance, but to beg.

I barely started to say the Creed when the Voice asked something. I answered, then started again — another question. I started for the fourth, the fifth time...

I could not go on. All my guilt, my concentration of will broke. The Voice confused my thoughts. It would not let me finish my prayers, It distracted me with Its questions. Then that infernal music surrounded me again with its whistles, flutes, organs... forming into words:

"You will die!"

* * *

"I want to confess!"

I called the guard for the second time that day. I knew: they wanted my confession upstairs. I didn't know whether the Voice had notified them through a secret gadget, or whether It could give orders through mere power of suggestion.

My decision was firm: I will confess everything, all my sins. The service of the Truth Machine can begin only through my first voluntary step.

I paced up and down for hours and could barely wait for the great moment. Finally in the afternoon the guard came for me. I knew where we were going: the Voice told me. I found Its knowledge of everything around me natural. It saw everything that happened, the rooms, the stairs.

Upstairs in the interrogation room the captain waited in uniform.

"You want to confess?" he asked. Apparently the guard had told him of my intention.

"Yes, Captain. I want to confess my sins."

"Your sins?"

He reached for the phone, dialed, then put the receiver on the table. I lifted my head to hear the Voice better.

I had rehearsed in my mind so freqently how I would list my sins, I merely needed an opening: "Free of all force and influence," I started as if I were reading it, "without being questioned, I want to confess the sins of all my life... " I stopped. "Life confession," that was the correct word! My conscience forced me to confess, not the AVH. I must serve truth, that will cleanse my soul.

The captain did not interrupt.

"I committed my first sin as a small child. I stole a stamp from my friend's album when I was 7 or 8. As my second sin I organized a fight at school when I was 11. My troop attacked the other troop of the class. Later I made fun of my Italian teacher. I did not share my lunch with a classmate who had only a slice of bread to eat.

The captain did not speak.

"Get to the war!" the Voice urged.

"How about the university years?" I worried.

"Later! Hurry! During the war... "

I swallowed, then started in a hoarse voice: "The Russians are a benevolent Slavic people. They shared with me even their last potato. They regarded me a fellow human being, not an enemy soldier. I took a water-boiler from an old Jewish woman. She had three, I had none. A soldier can be cruel when he is hungry. I collected Soviet insignia. I gave them bread in return, but I know now, I should have given the bread away, without asking for anything in return. I used to exchange my surplus for icons as well, but I had not done it from the goodness of my heart..."

The Voice carefully followed every sentence. Occasionally It interrupted me, if, on account of cowardliness, I had not used the right expression to show the true extent of my greed.

It took a long time to enumerate everything, but the Captain had not interrupted me once. When I finished, he hung up the receiver and stood up: "Go back to your cell!"

The guard did not handcuff me. They both understood I was on my way to becoming a better person. They sensed I no longer considered them evil.

The Voice was right yet again: no-one was truly evil.

* * *

I heard peculiar noises. Doors slammed, boots trampled, people chatted. Their voices drifted through my ears. I could not understand the meaning of their words. Yet, I sensed they talked about me. Someone sighed: "The unfortunate fellow! I feel really sorry for him!"

Sorry for me? Where did this all come from? The AVH required strict silence in this building. The noise could not have come from the street though, the tightly sealed windows locked out any outside sounds. It must have come from the hall. Who could be sorry for me?

The Voice reminded me of the AVH lieutenant. When I last saw him, he seemed nicer, more polite. He actually told me: "I chased you all over Budapest. I knew where you were every minute. They wanted you dead or alive. I could have shot you. I waited until you went to Lake Balaton — and only then did I arrest you."

I forgave him for his rudeness, I started to like his face with the pronounced Tartar cheekbones. Was he at fault for awkwardly trampling over people's lives now and then? He was merely following his conscience, searching for truth.

Certainly, truth stood behind the Voice. One puzzle remained: did the AVH have any connection with the Voice? It occurred to me that the Voice might be the head of the AVH.

"Can I be Gabor Peter?" said the Voice.

"No!... At least I don't think so," I tried to rule out this possibility as nonsense.

"And why not? Don't beat around the bush! Say it!" It read my thoughts about Gabor Peter, an uneducated, morally despicable man.[1] It continued: "You are right, I am not Gabor Peter."

"Why must I believe that all people are good?"

No answer, only a repeat of its truth-axiom: "Look for good in others and for the bad in yourself."

---

[1] Gabor Peter organized the AVH as brigadier-general. In May of 1949, as Chief of the AVH, he was promoted to lieutenant-general. Arrested January 1, 1953, he received a life term in 1955.

I thought all statesmen, ministers, politicians, all officials in public life might well benefit from a similar examination of conscience. A soul-refresher course like this certainly might prompt them to new thoughts, new directions. People's preoccupation concerned only their bodies. I felt our souls deserved maintenance, cleansing, and periodic vacations as well. Was that the true meaning of confession?

Today the Voice did not compel me to ask for a beating; most of the night I stood at attention on top of my cot. The Voice straightened my fingers, adjusted my chest, stiffened my head.

"Are you crazy?" the singing sergeant asked. He stared up at me: "Why are you standing there, like some kind of spindle?"

I looked over his bald head without a word, at stiff attention.

"Do you hear?" he yelled at me. "Get off that bed, right now!"

I did not budge.

"Then stand there, you idiot!"

Later the Voice and I were still discussing matters. I lay wrapped in my blanket. At the clinking of keys I sat up on the cot. An AVH lieutenant came in. On his collar he wore the insignia of the medical core, white cross on a blue background. A doctor! He held a huge syringe in one hand. He put his fingers on his mouth ordering me to be quiet. "Don't be afraid!" he whispered. He lifted the blanket off my leg. I barely felt the tiny sting. He tiptoed out. I slept like a baby.

I woke to a roll of drums roaring right in my ear. Light, the color of lead, poured over the cell through the small window. The black and white stone tiles of the floor started to twirl.

They poisoned me! The entire cell moved. The doctor — what had he given me to invoke this? Or was it the Voice, mocking me again?

When the drum roll ended, a new confused choir started singing. I saw the color of the sounds, a whistling, roaring, flute-playing Black Requiem. A melody of many parts developed. A song, a woman's **voice, gave me hope: "Don't be afraid! Don't be afraid!" she kept repeating.**

A deep voice sang in rounds with her prodding: "You must die... You must die!"

My head spun and my body shook in response to the varying pro**mises and threats until, finally, the choir dissolved into the hum of the waterpipe-web.**

* * *

The blond captain offered me a seat and took the receiver off the hook.

"It records your confession," the Voice reminded me. "Spoil it by saying every word twice, then repeat every sentence."

The captain asked me not to talk about my sins, but about my case. He wanted to hear about the conspiracy.

"You may do so," the Voice agreed. "But, don't forget the repetitions."

I started my speech: "In the summer... in the summer... of nineteen forty-eight... of nineteen forty-eight... I met... I met... "

The captain showed no surprise. Generally speaking I gave him the same confession I already had.

"Thank you, that will do!" the captain interrupted and replaced the receiver.

The Voice praised me for my performance because the recording could not be used for anything, but I had my doubts. It puzzled me why my invisible partner considered everyone good, while reality was often evil. Did the AVH have the right to pursue truth indiscriminately, whatever the means? How could the AVH be both good and bad at the same time? Why did the Voice demand I mock this horrifying authority?

Many things I could not see clearly.

The dusk of the evening beautified everything, I let myself into the world of fantasy where obstacles, guards and borders dissolved. There, no power, no authority could prevent me from doing as I pleased.

I barely stepped across the threshold of my imaginary world when a full-bodied, square-shouldered civilian entered my cell and jerked me back into reality. Behind him stood eight AVH officers with sparkling epaulets.

These men would not hurt me. I trusted the Voice. The sight of so many officers filled me with a sense of importance. I waited calmly.

The civilian walked around my cell and pointed to a brown spot on the wall, blood from my wounded head, or maybe my bloody fingerprint.

"What is this?" he asked.

"I don't know."

His look searched the empty cell. He slowly went to the door, then stopped on the threshold.

"Is it true you often don't eat your food? Do you get too much?"

"I don't get too much, but I punish myself," I answered proudly.

"Watch out!" said the Voice. "Your life is at stake. You must pretend to be mad! Don't let him leave! Yell after him: 'Mister Chief Executive'!"

I yelled loudly, sternly, as the Voice commanded. The man, built like an athlete, jumped right at me and hit me hard across the face. I was shocked. Nothing had prepared me for that.

"Don't worry about it!" the Voice calmed me. "Now you see what kind of good man he is? Continue!"

"Mister Chief Executive!" I repeated, shouting.

He delivered two more blows. My ears buzzed, but what hurt most was that my trust was thoroughly shaken by this procedure.

"Why are you yelling, you bastard?... Are you pretending to be crazy?" the giant's face turned beet-red while he yelled.

Why did the man behave like that? I believed him to be good and understanding. His blows did not hurt half as much as his words.

Puzzled, I watched them leave.

I forgot them fast when my invisible friend led me back to the world of fantasy. We prepared for a great showcase trial to culminate in an all-out ideological battle between East and West. On whose side would truth stand?

All showcase trials, were alike: the broken, glass-eyed Cardinal Mindszenty[2] received the same treatment as did the ascetic well-groomed Rajk[3], or Archbishop Groz[4] This one would be no different.

As always: the accused, the accusers, the judges, the lawyers and the assigned defense all appear in order. Only this time the Voice would be on our side.

So be it! This time, let the deceit, lies, or truth of the West be unearthed. This time, let the denial and truth-twisting of the East be discovered. The Voice will be the only true defender. It will be my helpmate when the rehearsed, dime-a-dozen confessions start, offsprings of death threats.

I see the first accused: he wears a dress suit, the perfect costume to appear in the drama staged for the world press. The AVH officer who accompanies the pale, frightened man gives him a last reminder as he steps before the stage lights: "All depends on you alone. If you don't perform properly we will hang you."

The accused confesses to perfection.

Suddenly the Voice interrupts the theatrical performance. The accused understands, someone can read his thoughts. He becomes frightened. He is shocked by the diabolical joke. Then he realizes: all this happens in the interest of Truth. He receives strength from the unknown Voice. He no longer worries about threats or consequences.

---

[2]Cardinal Mindszenty was Primate of Hungary. He was arrested December 26, 1948, and tried for conspiracy on February 2, 1949. He was sentenced to life imprisonment.

[3]Laszlo Rajk was Minister of the Interior, later Minister of Foreign Affairs of the Communist government. He was sentenced to death September 24, 1949 and was immediately executed. The system rehabilitated him in 1956, before the Revolution.

[4]Archbishop Grosz was the successor of the imprisoned Cardinal Mindszenty. The trials of his conspiracy case started in January of 1951. He himself was arrested May 15, 1951. In June he was sentenced to life imprisonment.

The prosecutor turns in shame: his thoughts are also read. The president of the council gets confused and becomes unable to interrupt the trial, or to give any orders.

A horrifying sense of inferiority pervades those who held the demonic rein of power in their hands, with such tremendous security, only minutes before. No turning back now. The Voice stands up against the Demon.

I felt comforted by this possibility, even if it was only a supposition, a hope, a dream...

THE SOUL FREEZES

End of October, 1952

The blond captain took off my handcuffs.

"Well," he started.

I did not sit down, but stepped to him, as the Voice commanded. I whispered into his ear: "The special group commands that you should not make them take me, captain!"

"All right!" he whispered back.

"Now I will not confess anything!"

"Fine with me, if that's what you want."

The guard clipped my handcuffs back on and returned me to my cell.

As soon as the hallway was quiet again, the Voice and I discussed the collaborators of the Truth Machine.

It was not easy for that contraption to choose completely truthful people. People of truth were the only ones who could be servers of the World Power of Truth. Constant research went on, even among the leaders of the Soviet State.

That Italian scientist who had escaped from America... or was it Great Britain?... could he have been the Voice? Impossible. The Voice knew the Hungarian conditions to their tiniest details... and the language!

Was it possible to read thoughts in different languages? How do the thoughts, expressed in different languages, become speech?

The Machine must have solved this problem: language is the only form of expression for thought. If the recording of thoughts is a mere recording of electrical vibrations, then those, in turn, can again be converted to any language.

The Voice merely said: "The time will come when we will be able to examine all human thought. The epoch of truth shall come when there will be no more liars."

"Not even Stalin?" the question flashed through me.

I could see the nasty old man clearly in my mind's eye. There was no aversion in me toward him, I saw him with the objectivity of a medical doctor.

"I give you great news!" the Voice announced. I heard the soft ring of a bell. Majestic, black drapery surrounded a big coffin, lying in state. Slowly they lowered the coffin.

"What is this?" I asked the Voice.

"Stalin will die... He will be murdered!"

"When?"

"A couple of months, maybe half a year from now. Mark today's date."

Date? Why would the date be important for me? How could I have known what day it was: Monday, or Friday? The fifteenth, or the first?

"What do you think the date is today? What month?"

I tried to calculate the weeks, the months, but I had no set point in time to help me. A number fell in front of my eyes, as if from a giant calendar. "21 October."

"October 21... 1952!" I answered deliberately. Stalin will be dead in six months. The terrible secret ran through my mind; with Stalin dead, a million things will collapse. Every joint may give way in that giant empire the old man held together with his extraordinary iron will. I came back to my essential question. Was he a good man or an evil one?

Should I believe he wanted the good of his people? Did he indeed build a "truth-village" in the foothills of the Ural? The Voice told me, "Stalin gave them everything. He wanted to conduct an experiment. He tore one million people out of the Russian body: families, children. He gave them everything: family homes, dachas with gardens multiplied like mushrooms. The only rule was that everyone had to tell the truth." Had this research evoked smiles and happiness, creative mood and peace? Had this peace created an atmosphere in which no-one sermonized about Communism or talked about Western democracy? The only rule was: everyone had to tell the truth. Especially the part that said "sermonizing about Communism or Western Democracies was not permitted," struck me as humorous. Logically this meant that maybe Stalin was not an evil man after all.

"Did he really build that village?" the Voice teased.

"I don't know."

In that moment, I no longer saw Stalin as evil, as a man who exiled, murdered and let people rot in concentration camps by the millions. "If he did indeed build a truth-village... "

I was sorry for the man. Violent death awaited him. The struggle between Beria and Kaganovich would flare up. What would Beria do with Stalin's exceptional reservation? That third man... what was his name? Something Mal... Malen... Malenkov.

"Come," the guard's voice brought me back from my far-reaching daydreams.

He moved me to another cell. It was simple; I had no physical things to move. My new cell faced the guard's room and looked similar to the other one. The light barely flickered, while the lights in the other cells glared with blinding 100 Watt bulbs. Did they want to protect me from becoming blind? Maybe they rewarded me for telling the truth.

"It will be warmer here," the guard explained slamming the door, without waiting for thanks.

I heard someone empty coal into a stove. My worn jacket kept me warm enough. But compared to the adventures introduced into my life by the Voice, the importance of starvation or cold dwindled to nothing.

I carried the terrifying choir with me to my new cell. The enormous pipes on the ceiling poured forth the requiem of the organs and whistles. Male and female voices sang: "You will die!... You will die!"

"Don't worry, you won't!" the Voice assured me; sometimes It was thin and high, other times a deep bass.

At times It called from behind my back, on other occasions It whistled from the ceiling: "Listen to me, I am the Good Voice!" Then from the other corner of the cell: "I am the Evil Voice!"

Good Voice!... Evil Voice! Which one should I believe? One threatens me with death, the other gives hope for life. What new diabolical invention was this? Did the Machine want to prove that good and bad both lived in every person? Devils and angels fought for my soul!

* * *

That same night the black-haired lieutenant interrogated me again. A civilian sat beside him. I had confessed to this lieutenant on the infamous night of my great mad scene. He laid the short report of my confession in front of me, then waited patiently for me to read it.

"Sign it on each page," he said after I returned the sheets.

The Voice, to my amazement, showed distrust and advised me to be cautious and trick my interrogators. It ordered me to sign my name in an unaccustomed, illegible, crooked way. I obeyed.

The lieutenant made no remarks. He stared at me with his sunken eyes: "Do you hear the Voice?" he asked.

His question took me by surprise. I could not have answered him if I wanted to. Was he, too, in on the secret of the "special troop"? Did he, too, know about my connection with the Voice?

He waited a while, then waved his hand.

"Well, all right, don't answer. Only don't say later that you signed this document in order to comply with the wishes of some celestial Voice!"

"I told the truth, lieutenant!"

"Fine. I hope some day we'll play bridge together," he said, winking his eye.

His last sentence haunted me. How did he know I liked to play bridge?

Downstairs, the Voice absolved me from asking to be hit, but I had to fast.

The next day at the shower stalls the opera-humming sergeant on duty behaved in the friendliest way. He did not touch me, even when I asked for a slap across the face.

Putting down the thoroughly wet towel, I heard the Voice's order boom at me: "Ask to go to the restroom! Then demand to be locked into the punishment cell, the one the small Greek man mentioned. Do you remember him? The short French teacher, from Greece?"

Of course I remembered the strange man in his grey ethnic clothes. He spent a few nights in my cell about two months ago. The sergeant with the operatic aspirations immediately let me go to the bathroom. On my way back I stopped in front of him.

"Sir, lock me into the punishment cell."

"Where?"

"Into that tiny concrete cell."

"There is no such thing here."

"But I know there is. I demand to be locked there."

"Stop talking nonsense and get back to your cell!"

"I won't."

He looked at me, stupefied. He tried to push me towards my cell: "Get!"

"No!"

He grabbed my arm and tried to drag me. I resisted because the Voice wanted me to get acquainted with the punishment cell.

I slid from the sergeant's grip, but he caught me in the narrow hallway and pushed me through the cell door.

When the big door slammed shut behind me, I remembered the concrete cell... and the tiny Greek.

* * *

One night a long time ago, in August of 1952, when I had already spent about a month in jail, I heard the key rattle. I turned to the door, rigid with fear.

A short man in grey overalls entered.

He turned towards the wall as if he were admiring the perfect whitewash. I threw off my blanket and approached him. I was not afraid of him, although I knew he was a spy for the AVH. I fought back my distrust and introduced myself, giving him a hearty handshake.

He was embarrassed and murmured something.

"How did you get in here?" I said. I had already decided, if he was indeed a spy for the AVH, he was a clumsy one.

"I worked in a quarry!" he answered in pain.

"Why did they arrest you?"

"They accused me of sabotage. Two of the trams ran into each other and they made me responsible for the accident."

His story may have been true, the powers looked for sabotage even in the laws of gravity, yet I didn't trust the man.

"Sit down," I motioned him to the cot.

I glanced at his shoes, black, worn workboots, the laces missing — no socks. He caught my glimpse.

"You were allowed to keep your socks?" he asked.

"Yes. Why?"

"When people get here, they take away their socks and remove all the iron taps from their shoes."

"Not with me they didn't."

"That's funny," he said shaking his head. He chewed at his mouth as if in deep thought. Two enormous golden teeth flashed at me.

"Have you been working in the mines for long?" I started again.

"About two years."

I scrutinized his worn work clothes, his stocky crossed legs, his calloused hands, his gold teeth.

The keys rattled again. The sergeant came back. I thought of him as "Goldie" since he "forgot" to take my gold watch to inventory and promised to smuggle out my poem. He stepped to my new companion and tugged at his jacket.

"Well, squash-head, when will they hang you?"

Anger spread over the short man's face: "I don't think they will, Sir."

"You don't think so, eh?"

The sergeant punched him in the chest, with the playful evilness of a lion toying with its prey. The tiny man backed all the way to the wall to regain his balance. His face betrayed the helplessness of repressed anger.

"Are you learning the language?" the sergeant turned to me.

"What language?" I asked.

"French, this squash-head speaks French. Don't you?" the sergeant addressed me, but turned to his victim and grabbed the edge of his jacket.

I looked at my companion with surprise.

85

"He hasn't told you yet?" the sergeant did not want to believe his ears.

"No!"

"He had to know the language well enough. He was a French teacher."

Without a word I kept watching the frozen wrinkles on the prisoner's face that expressed his internal anger.

"It's true, squash-head, ain't it, you were a French teacher?" the sergeant poked him again.

"True."

"And how did you like it there, in Greece?" another punch accompanied the question.

The outside railings of the prison rattled, steps approached and finally reached the cell. The slim blond sergeant appeared.

"Come!" he waved to my companion who left the room with visible relief.

In all probability the short "Greek" was taken for questioning. In prison nicknames were acquired easily. To me this short man would always remain the "Greek." For the life of me I couldn't figure out why he had been to Greece, or how he had managed to get to the cellar of the AVH by teaching French.

Goldie wanted to talk. He opened my food-window.

"How do you make out with the little 'Greek'?" he inquired. He used the same nickname.

"Sir, he just came a few minutes ago."

"You will be pretty tight, the two of you on the same cot."

"Will he stay with me?"

"Maybe."

I had mixed feelings. The strange little man meant novelty, adventure after the loneliness. Silence populates the cell with shadows, induces worry. At least we were not forbidden to talk.

"Come here!" Goldie lowered his voice. I went close to the window. "I took the letter!" he whispered.

"What letter?"

"The one you sent to your wife, the poem."

This AVH sergeant took a poem to my wife — impossible. I assumed he only promised to do it in order to calm his conscience for adopting my gold watch.

"Thank you, Sir," I answered unconvinced and suspicious. Was he rude to the Greek only to show me how cruel he could be to those with no watch to "adopt"?

He still stood in front of the food-window, waiting for something.

"Why did they bring him to my cell?" I asked, only to satisfy his expectation.

He hesitated for an instant, then answered: "No room in the other cells."

He lied. Every morning I counted the mess-kits in front of the cells. There were seven for fourteen cell doors. His lie was stupid which made it more intriguing. What could the real reason be for moving the "Greek" in with me?

"Where did they take the little 'Greek'?" I kept prodding.

"To the concrete cell."

"Where?"

"The standing cell. There is room for one man, standing up. Water drips on him constantly."

"Why was he locked there?"

"He must have lied."

The sergeant locked the window. He lied too. Here everyone was either accusing you with lying, lying himself, or both.

When they returned the small "Greek" he looked no different. I whispered my questions late that night: "Did they torture you? Was it bad?"

"What?"

"The standing cell."

"What standing cell?"

"Where they took you. The standing cell with the dripping water?"

"What are you talking about?" He was mad. "They did not take me to any standing cell and they have not tortured me."

He rose up on his elbow: "Where did you get this nonsense?"

His vehement denial surprised me. I did not want to betray Goldie. I regarded him as my accomplice ever since he had told me about the poem.

"I haven't heard from anybody," I retreated, "I only thought they gave you a bad time. You were away for so long."

"I had to write!" was his terse answer.

One of them had lied: either he, or the sergeant.

I could not fall asleep. The cot was narrow for one person, let alone two. I lay on my back to avoid his breath.

"You are not sleeping," he stated rather than asked. "Why don't you put your hands on top of the blanket," he continued, "like you are supposed to?"

"Why?"

"Didn't they tell you? It's the rule."

The small opening on the door flipped open and the light of the hallway flashed into the cell for an instant.

"That bastard," the Greek whispered. I realized he was referring to Goldie, remembering the earlier punches. "Did he hurt you?"

"No, not me."

"If he touches me once more I'll report him," the Greek vowed.

I broke the uneasy silence with a question that had bothered me all day. "Why did they put us together?"

"I don't know."

We lay there in silence, but the secret of the Greek teacher would not let me rest. I learned he gave French lessons in Greece and came back to Hungary in 1949. Greek troops annihilated Markos' troops in 1949 and the Communists had to run for their lives. Had he been involved in that? Was he being punished for failure? He talked noncommittally about the physical labor they compelled him to do after his return home.

They called him out several times during the day. Even if he was a spy, he could not have said much about me. I was convinced of one thing: he was dead set on reporting Goldie and unafraid of any revenge.

After a while they took the little "Greek" away and I never saw him again.

* * *

The clinking of the coal-shovel brought me back to the ice cold present. Even the guard was cold, he kept stacking his stove with coal. Though I could hear the sound of heat I could not feel its warmth.

I heard again the voice of Mr. Maros, the lawyer. He, too, must have been cold because he asked the guard to let him sit beside the stove. During his interrogation I imagined his bearded face and bent shoulders as he crouched down to the stove in his overalls and clapping clogs. His voice sounded content. He could absorb some warmth while the guard questioned him.

Mr. Maros said something like "he's crazy." Who was this miserable guy talking about? Who went crazy?

I heard his clogs clop-clop back to the cell, then silence enveloped the prison again.

Timeless time continued. Day and night melted into one; nothing broke the circular motion of the endless cycle. My only companion, the music of the pipes, alternately sent me into desperation or gave me hope.

A new Voice sounded distinctly over the choir constantly reminding me to tell the truth. It confused me by arguing one instant as the "Good Voice," the next as the "Evil Voice," claiming Evil would win in the end.

Which one should I believe? Which voice should I follow? Whose orders were right?

I felt I must repent for my sins, ask for more punishment; I demanded isolation. The singer who took me to the bathroom that morning only shook his head at me and pushed me into the shower. While I was listening to the whisper of the water from the tap, I conceived my new plan. I won't return to my cell. I will stay in the hallway, again. This time it will work! I stepped out of the bathroom and stood in front of the folding cot where the empty mess kits were stored. I stubbornly counted the mess kits as if I had all the time in the world.

"What are you waiting for?" the sergeant pushed me. "Why don't you go back to your cell?"

"I won't go back."

"What do you think you are doing?"

"I want you to punish me."

"Don't be an ass."

He pulled me, but I grabbed the iron bed. We fought. The mess kits crashed onto the stone floor. This brought out the "Fang" from the guard's room. He tried to calm me while the guard disappeared, returning with a billy club. Blow after blow showered onto my hand holding the iron bed. I ignored it. The Voice commanded me to resist.

All in vain... there were two of them. They tore my hands off the bed and dragged me into the cell.

* * *

They led me to a round-faced second lieutenant I had never seen before. The big-boned young man asked his irrelevant questions in a bored tone; about food, bathing, as if my health were his only concern. He finished his questions with: "Please, now, try to answer concisely."

Wasn't I answering concisely? His questions were not only simple, they were primitive. If I took too long answering, it was because I waited for instructions from the Voice.

"Concentrate now... " he warned. "Don't you feel weak?"

Of course I did! My knees shook, I was freezing and tired. He did not keep me for long.

The next day he had a long questionnaire in front of him. He wrote down my answers while he paced the cell with awkward, leaden steps. This spiritual inventory — which could not even be called an interrogation — thoroughly confused me.

An unusual smell greeted me in the hall adding to my confusion. I could not decide whether the odor reminded me of a cleaner or a disinfectant. Could it have been some strange powder that caused my weakness?

I finally dismissed this idea. After all, the guards all breathed the same air.

An ugly civilian in a rain-coat visited my cell. I felt hostility for no apparent reason. Where did instinctive antipathy originate? Why was I unjust with this newcomer? He had not been asked by Providence what kind of looks he wanted.

With no intentions of harming me, he walked to the middle of the cell in complete silence. I followed the rules and greeted him with a "Good day." I forced myself to be objective.

He returned my greeting politely and asked how I felt. What else could I have answered? I assured him I was all right. The constant **questions about my health started to bother me. They certainly did not worry about how the beatings affected my well being.**

He looked me up and down: "Is the food enough?"

I waited for the Voice. It urged me to tell the truth. "It isn't much!"

"Not much?" his thin eyebrows, pulled into a pointed arc, **reminded me of a bird of prey.**

"Not much!" I repeated. "Mostly I get soup."

"You don't even eat what you get."

That stopped me. He was right.

After this irrelevant visit the guard came in. He had a billy club in his hand. He slowly walked the length of the cell, his eyes on me. "Good afternoon. Why did you scribble all over the door?" he asked.

Since Goldie had been arrested I had not even seen a pencil. He had smuggled in a tiny pencil and paper so I could write that poem. Since then — how could anyone have had a pencil without permission?

"I haven't scribbled anything, Mr. Inspector," I answered, embarassed. "I don't have anything with which to scribble."

"Don't lie!"

"I am not lying."

"Then who drew those windmills on the door?"

"Windmills... on the door?"

I didn't look. Even if there were mills there someone else had done it.

"If I catch you drawing something on the bed, or the wall," — he swung the billy club at me — "I wouldn't want to be in your shoes... "

I stared after him incredulously. This young man was never bad with me. He hit me only when I demanded it.

I had no time for meditation. They led me to the tall second lieutenant. Through his window I could see the yard. The sun glistened on the branches of the immense, leafless wild chestnut tree.

He put paper and pen in front of me: "Write down the story of your life."

A simple task; in the Communist system they always started with: "write down the story of your life." I began with my birth: "I was born in a petit bourgeois family." Three categories of descent were acceptable: proletarian, peasant, or petit bourgeois. The worst was of course petit bourgeois, but no one would go beyond that. I was convinced even princes and counts wrote "Petit bourgeois." I found it ironic that we had never placed more emphasis on descent than in this society of equality.

This time the Voice made me write "bourgeois," telling me to leave out "petit" as that would be a lie. Someone had to call himself "bourgeois" to represent the 3 million Hungarian bourgeoisie.

I wrote diligently about the social and literary involvement of my youth and got to the days of my law practice when the Voice came up with a bizarre idea. It interrupted my train of thought because it wanted to know whether I could entertain several topics simultaneously. My hand stopped.

The second lieutenant rose from the table.

"I see you are tired! That's enough for today," he paused: "Maybe you'll be taken to Budapest."

My knees started shaking. He noticed it.

"Are you afraid of something?" he asked.

"No! I'm just weak," I confessed. It was not true. I was deadly afraid of a trip to Budapest.

"I guess I may even count on the worst punishment," I said cautiously. I dreaded to mention "death."

"I don't think so," he said. "Archbishop Grosz had also committed serious crimes, yet his punishment amounted to no more than 12 years."

Twelve years! I should be so lucky!

The Voice asked me how I would feel if my older daughter visited me with a bouquet of flowers. I hoped it would be a reward for my telling the truth.

I believed this so strongly that in the afternoon when the guard took me up again, I was convinced my daughter would fly into my arms. I was so involved in my fantasy I even forgot to knock on the door according to rules. The guard was shocked, but said nothing.

The second lieutenant was alone in the room. The Voice had deceived me!

I continued writing the story of my life. I ignored the Voice and finished quickly.

The Voice did not follow me into my cell. Only the choir expected me, spelling out my fate in loud screams: "You have to die." Its strict whispering, squealing, trilling melody repeated late into the night: "You will die!"

Maybe so, but I was also aware of the innumerable tortures I might have to endure before I died.

The next day I went to be interrogated again. The second lieutenant said: "You will be going soon. Higher authorities will question you. I want to warn you: in your own interest... keep your answers short. If you talk too much you might hurt others as well as yourself."

His advice surprised me. Until now, everyone wanted me to talk more, more, more. This was the first one of my captors who gave me doubts about the wisdom of always telling the truth.

I didn't know what to answer. Strong self-accusations welled up in me despite the fact that I merely followed the Voice's orders when I told all. What kind of troubles had I triggered for others? Maybe I shouldn't have talked when no one had asked me.

The Voice returned to me only in the cell. It assured me: justice would win.

THEY ARE TAKING ME TO BUDAPEST

Beginning of November 1952

Chills ran up and down my spine as I huddled on the cot, while the choir repeated the second lieutenant's words over and over again: "They'll take you!"

The Evil Voice screamed at me mockingly, like the witch in my childhood nightmares: "You will die!" The Good Voice promised life and justice. An ant's hill of thoughts worked in my head as the guard led me out to the yard. He handcuffed me. Two soldiers with submachine guns stood by my side. Several AVH men cleaned a truck in the yard. The guards led me to a brown luxury Pobeda passenger car.

"Sit in the middle, in the back!" an unknown officer commanded. I sat, squeezed between two soldiers, on the back seat.

I turned around curiously looking for cables. If the Machine was in the hands of the AVH, there should be some evidence of it.

"What are you looking for?" the officer screamed at me.

I could not betray the Voice.

The car swerved into the traffic of the city. My eyes drank in the sight of people, of houses. The pedestrians turned from the car loaded with AVH policemen. How could they have known it was carrying a man condemned to die, his death announced by the screaming, screeching pipe-music. An eerie silence reigned in the car as it reached the highway and zoomed ahead. It slowed down as it passed a cart loaded with the season's late hay. I looked into the face of the man sitting on the cart.

All men looked forward to life... I alone faced death. Everyone anticipated seeing the sun next day, only I would never see it again. How cruel it was to show the glitter and beauty of life to someone marching to his death. The rolling hills of Transdanubia beckoned, the morning smell of hay lured me, the few human words I could hear, the friendly greetings people exchanged, the steam emanating from the bodies of the horses; all called to life. That temptation was torture.

I lifted my hand in front of a roadside crucifix. "Don't make the sign of the cross on your stomach!" one of the soldiers mocked. Whether or not he was mocking, he was right. I could easily have lifted my hand to my head and heart. Why hadn't I? Did I feel awkward? Was I afraid?

The pain of life waiting for death became more acute as we passed the cozy, middle class cities, long rows of locust trees bordering the road, the opaque green lakeshore of Balaton, the familiar hill of Martonvasar, the orchards of Erd, the highway along the Danube. Finally we arrived in the capital city, Budapest, with its clinking streetcars, honking automobiles, reek of gas and chemicals yet the whole city was laced with parks and fountains.

I had not an inkling where I would end up.

We crossed the Danube and were speeding towards Rakoczi Ave. Whenever we stopped at a red light it seemed that the drivers of the other cars cast secret glances at us. Then with feigned indifference, they would hunch over their steering wheels. Had they noticed the prisoner in the back seat?

I had an awful premonition: the Voice had disappeared. Yet I knew it would be there again, whenever I needed It. It promised.

"Jump out!" the officer ordered and grabbed my handcuffs. We stood in front of a tiny door in the middle of a busy street. A gold lapeled AVH policeman opened the door. A grill shut behind us. We found ourselves in a well-lit corridor. We didn't have to wait long. Another officer came to get me. He held on tightly to a filefolder.

"Do you remember me?" he asked, smiling slightly.

He was the one who told me "You will tell all before long, just like Mindszenty." He watched me, quite pleased with himself, as I followed the guard like a sleepwalker. We went down a long flight of stairs and arrived in a cellar corridor. Innumerable pipes ran along the ceiling. We treaded on red, worn matting. The small cells on the right hand side of the hallway must have been coal bins at one time. One of the doors opened.

The space measured a few square yards. Two wooden cots with a concrete base occupied almost the entire cell.

"Cadaver cell!" I said under my breath and fell onto the cot.

Fear of dying and hunger battled in me. One affected the spirit, the other — the flesh.

At least they might feed me before the hanging. I did not want to break down under the hanging tree, I did not want them to see me afraid; afraid — not as much of death, but of losing my life. Maybe I could gain a few months, a few weeks. At least it was warm here. I longed for some soup and bread.

I had not noticed I was actually moaning the words under my breath. A strong lightbulb glared over the cell door. On the cellar wall, brown stains colored the old, worn and dirty whitewash. I found a big cross, drawn by pencil, and another, smaller one. There a third one could be traced... and inscriptions, names. "God be with you, Mother," "I will die," "Murderers." Many of these hieroglyphs of the condemned I could not read. This might be my last contact with earth.

It was impossible to pace in the approximately one square yard of space left between the cot and the door.

The guard put a mess-tin on the floor in front of me.

"Take it!" he snapped.

A big piece of bread accompanied the steaming creamed peas. I fell onto the bread like a prey bird on its victim and mauled it. The hunger of several months demanded satisfaction. I finished quickly, although I wanted to prolong every minute, to revel in the joy of eating. I was extending life — eating meant life. The food was hot and edible! Yet, death was waiting at the door. The pipes even in this new place continued their joy-defeating choir: "You will die." I no longer cared what the pipe-music might say, I covered my eyes and leaned against the wall. The darkness soothed me.

The Voice surprised me with its sudden presence: "Did you miss me? I told you I would return. Did you believe me?"

I nodded, more out of custom than enthusiasm.

"Do you hear the screaming?"

Although the buzzing sound of the choir bothered me, I could hear the moaning, or screaming, even through my blunted, faint senses. "I hear it."

"Don't believe it. It isn't real."

"What is it then?"

"A recording. These people are not that bad."[1] True, they did not hurt me. Did the Voice's repeated instructions mean I could believe everyone? Should I dare something new for the sake of justice? Should I make the Chief of the AVH swear he, too, was able to tell the truth?

But how? An atheist cannot swear on the Bible! Could he be persuaded to swear on the "health of his family?" I wanted to make him swear he would tell the truth under the supervision of the soul-reading Machine.

Truth won under any conditions. I had my reward for being truthful: warm cell, steaming vegetables, a bigger piece of bread.

---

[1]The AVH perfected the torturing methods of the Gestapo. One spiritual torture was the "record" questioning. The person to be questioned was made to believe that next door his/her dependent or relative was being tortured and confessing. Allegedly that person was screaming. In reality it was a record.

I AM WRITING

Beginning of November, 1952

The guard did not handcuff me this time, he just pointed towards the cellar stairs. The long upstairs corridor was essentially the main floor and on the same level as the street. A man with a pointed chin, dressed in civilian clothes, awaited me in the interrogation room. He sat stiffly behind his desk. Pointing awkwardly at the chair he gruffed: "Sit down!"

The Voice was curious whether I could guess his rank: captain? major? first lieutenant?

A tiny jolt compelled me to answer: "Lieutenant."

Startled, he lifted his head: "What makes you think I am a lieutenant?"

I could not tell him the Voice suggested it. I could not talk about the existence of the Machine either. Lying was out of the question.

"I guessed it!" I finally forced myself to answer.

"Call me, 'Sir'." He slowly pulled out a drawer and took out some kind of cracker. The Voice wondered whether he would offer me some. He didn't. He slowly gnawed at it, like a fat white mouse.

"You all always expect the Messiah!" he started in a measured tone. "You were expecting the fall of the dictatorship of the proletariat. You discussed it at your card parties, you chatted about it in the hallways of the court houses, you made remarks about it at the gatherings of the Catholic Circle. That was the reason why you wanted to go to the West: you couldn't wait. So, WE came instead of the Messiah. There are many who try to escape to the West. First we forgive them and they can redeem themselves through a lengthy prison sentence. Then they try a second time. By that time they usually spy against us. Then, instead of the Messiah, they receive a 'tie' around their necks."

The Voice did not interrupt.

"You find yourself in the same situation!" he continued. "We know you were waiting for the change, the Messiah. What kind of sentence do you expect?"

I had to face reality, but the straightforward question made me uncertain. Everyone would shrink from declaring the death sentence onto himself. Should I say death? Or life? I listened for the Voice's advice.

"Strict sentence!" I answered, avoiding finality.

"Yes. But that depends on you as well; on how you behave with authorities."

I thought I had always behaved in an exemplary way; I had behaved neither stubbornly nor rudely. I myself asked for punishment, for slaps. How could I have behaved badly in prison?

"Do as you are told by the guards. Do not disturb the peace, do not shout and don't be impatient."

Only a madman would resist the inside order of prison. I certainly would not.

"You will receive pencil and paper," he changed the subject.

Would that mean a betterment of my condition? I hoped that the privilege of receiving pencil and paper would not lead to my death.

"Pencil and paper," he repeated, "Inasmuch as you have something to note, something you will want to tell us... I will give you some small, insignificant homework as well. Write down the names of all your friends and everything you know about them. Do you understand?"

"In a political sense?" I asked at the urging of the Voice.

"In every sense," he answered, smiling. "Just write down everything you think important about them. We won't influence you. Naturally, what interests us most is their connection with your case, with the conspiracy."

I understood, I didn't even find it surprising. What else would they want to know but the truth? They had already investigated everything, anyway.

"Investigated everything" — this thought uncovered a peculiar contradiction. If they had to investigate, then the miraculous Machine could not have been in their possession.

Despite the Voice's allegations, that I was in the hands of good people, the knowledge that they were not identical with the Machine comforted me.

The Voice laughed at my thought. Its incomprehensible laughter accompanied me down the corridor, all the way to my cell, while the pipe-choir assured me, once again: "You will not die."

A mess-tin sat on my bed with two huge slices of bread. I almost hit the ceiling when I saw the tin's content. White noodles, covered with deliciously sauteed cabbage laughed at me from the dish. I gulped it down. Suddenly I felt so full I could not eat the two huge slices of bread. I parted from them with a sad heart when the guard finally took them.

"Tomorrow you will only get half!" he barked.

I laid the white paper and pencil beside me. I tried to befriend them. But, before I could write even as much as a sentence, the Voice grabbed me. It drew my attention to the sounds next door. Was that Palotai, the leader of our organization? As if he were talking to his cell-mate. I tried to understand the disjointed sentences, but every word whirled in an incomprehensible chaos. He contradicted, he discussed — I heard it in his voice — yet I had no idea what he was talking about. Was he addressing me?

I couldn't make up my mind, whether he had gone mad or whether the Machine was putting us in contact with each other through our thoughts. I had no right to suppose the Machine was working solely through me.

As far as I was concerned Palotai was making a fool of himself. He accused whoever sat beside me of being a spy. But nobody sat beside me. I stood as alone as the blinding lightbulb above the door. He said two people were sitting beside me. He ordered me to choke one of them to death that very night.

I jumped up. Had he gone crazy? What did he want from me? Who did they want choked? The music of the pipes swallowed my questions.

Palotai started his whispering again. I no longer knew if it was him, or Janosi, my doctor friend whom they took to the electric cell. Did he get out alive? Had they brought him here after his hospital stay?

Palotai had gone mad — fear struck me. Why torture him, while doing nothing to me? Why put people into electric cells to get the truth out of them if they had the Machine?

"Do you think they have it?" the Voice doubted. "Do you believe they possess the key to truth? Do you think Palotai talked with you? Maybe your imagination conjured up his voice."

I tore my hands away from my eyes and grabbed the pencil. I had to act, do something. I had to run from the whispering, screaming sounds of silence.

Silence in an AVH prison has its own sound, language, message. In silence everything takes on a form. Even the noise of a lone termite sounds like a gunshot. The frozen silence lets me hear the immeasurable noise of a silently opened door, suppressed moan, the trembling filament of the lightbulb, or the thousand-melodied choir of the damned waterpipes.

I escaped from the silence — into writing. My pencil ploughed a name into the paper: the name of the first friend that came to mind.

"Write the truth!" the Voice warned.

As long as I can write, I will live. The cell is warm and I can fill my stomach. I have reached the first level of life, that of animal instinct, but, nevertheless, life.

"Trust me!" the Voice said. "Maybe they won't harm you. Those who drew the black crosses on the wall did not yet know me. Our Machine had not existed then. Don't be afraid."

I wrote carefully so my writing would be clear and legible. I had always typed, writing by hand tired me easily. Now it served as a refuge from the monsters, the threat of death, the silence. I tried to organize my thoughts. My friend, the one whose name I had jotted down first, had a beard. Or had he shaved it? How could I forget whether my friend had had a goatee or not?

It didn't make any difference. My confession remained the same. I wrote about him honestly: he was a reactionary. He, I, and for that matter the whole country, were considered "reactionaries." We did not expect the dreams of the past to return, we looked for a rightful solution and humanitarian development. My friend was a member of the Communist Party, though that didn't count for much. Everyone knew, a former district judge may have joined the Party only for the sake of security.

I wrote the next name, then another one. The Voice giggled with me as I scribbled one name after another: the responsible official in **the ministry, the chief doctor at the hospital, the head of the accounting department, a judge, an attorney, and the police clerk.** They all play-acted. Public opinion accepted that some of them had joined the Party. They all became part of the deaf, invisible network which played the role of faithful adherents to the system.

"What are they going to say when they read this?" the Voice teased.

"They'll read this?" the pencil halted in my hand. "They said they already knew all this. My duty was merely to record the truth."

For the first time since my imprisonment the guard knocked on the cell door. A stocky sergeant appeared in the sharp flood of light. He looked like a peasant from Transdanubia. I just knew: he had to be a good man!

"What's all that you are writing?" he asked, bending over my papers. "Aren't you tired yet? It's almost morning."

"It feels good to write, sergeant," I answered pointing at the multiplying sheets on my cot.

He shook his head and locked my door again. His boots thumped on the matting as he walked down the corridor. I heard him spit and waited for the hiss of the next one.

"Aren't you sleepy yet?" the Voice inquired.

I shook my head "No." I racked my brain to remember who else's fate had ever intertwined with mine.

Finally: new names!

"What are they going to say..." the Voice laughed, "when they realize what a tremendous number of people whom they had trusted turned out to have been mere actors in order to survive?"

Its laughter was catching. I laughed so hard, my body shook.

"What are you laughing about, all on your own?" the sergeant asked, opening my door. "You like it here so much?"

I don't know whether I slept that night. The noise of breakfast dishes brought me back to reality. When I had to go to the bathroom, I knocked. A winding staircase took me to the main floor. We passed tiny cellar windows walled up tightly with tin. Sometimes a bit of outside light squeezed through its dusty slits.

During the interrogations the shades were always pulled. I could never figure out whether it was night or day outside. "Sir," as he asked to be addressed, looked embarrassed. He groped around in his drawer, but didn't pull anything out. I searched his face. I thought he had a blond goatee last time. Now he had none. Only his thin, pointed chin poked a hole into the air and reminded me of a sad goat. The only difference between a goat and this man was that the goat found grass, while he found nothing in his drawer. "Poor goat-man!"

The Machine — it made me laugh so much! What a powerful weapon! It would be a great solution to those ridiculous conferences where diplomats sit with straight faces through proposals that deserve nothing but mockery. This laughing-ray could relieve world tension!

"Do you want it now?" the Voice inquired.

"No... no... I beg you! Make him laugh, the goat-man."

Some force made me smile. The man's mouth twitched.

"What are you laughing at?" he asked seriously, as his office demanded.

"You don't dare to tell him how funny his goat-chin looks, eh?" the Voice teased.

Sir continued: "The guards reported how you laughed in your cell. I received your writing. You wrote a lot that does not interest us one bit."

"See?" the Voice continued to tease. "You wrote too much."

"Is your food enough?" the goat-chinned one interrupted.

"It is enough. Thank you."

"We have to clear up some questions. I hope you will tell the truth."

I frowned, wrinkling my forehead, hurt he would doubt my honesty.

He spread some paper on the table, opened his fountain pen and tried it. It ploughed into the paper noisily, then stopped abruptly in a fat inkspot.

"Ugly scene... " the Voice vexed me. "He has not even written anything, but he's already put his stamp on the document."

I pinched my knee so as not to laugh out loud.

"What do you know of your brother's spying in Yugoslavia?"

"Nothing!" I answered decisively, without waiting for the Voice's instructions.

"Don't lie!"

Scandalized, not comprehending, I kept my silence. How can this man attack me like that when he must know I didn't lie?

The Voice tried to explain: "Maybe he does not know everything, after all. Maybe he does not know about the Machine."

"Lieutenant," I said leaning forward in my chair. "I always tell the truth."

"I told you not to call me 'lieutenant'," he burst out. "Continue!"

"My brother escaped to Yugoslavia in 1949, but he never engaged in any intelligence activity. I can state that with the clearest conscience."

"You know," he looked through me as if I were transparent, "your religion does not serve to your advantage. But, if you behave yourself, you may escape this place without a 'tie' around your neck."

His words filled me with hope and happiness. I staggered after the guard with a radiant face. I will live, I will live, as the Voice promised.

"Look!" the Voice stopped at the bottom of the stairs. "Look what that skunk-faced sergeant is doing."

Skunkface held a bottle in his hand, pouring something into the mess-tins in front of him.

His hand stopped in mid-air as he noticed me.

"Get going, what are you staring at?" the guard pushed me along my way.

Soon the noisy, life-giving lunch arrived.

"What did he put in the food?" the Voice asked the question that kept me pondering whether Skunkface doctored the food with poison or vitamins.

The warmth of my cell and the food dispersed my fear. Whatever they put in the vegetables had no after-taste at all.

THE VOICE REVEALS ITSELF

Middle of November, 1952

What got into me? Suddenly I turned into a daredevil, a bragger. How could I even think of revealing this poem, THE poem? The Voice gave me courage, confidence to reveal all.

I sharpened my pencil, rubbing it on the cot and started writing: "The following poem is the creed of my oppositon to the Communist system... "

I knew it by heart, my pencil sped across the paper without hesitation.

HUNGARIAN SONG IN 1949

As once the last roused bison
On the harrassed borders of Transylvania
We stand, as lonely, as orphaned,
On the past and the threshold of great summits

"Are you writing a poemá" the spitting sergeant asked, opening my door. He bent over to see the letters. "Are you some kind of a writer?"

"Yes."

"May I get a new pencil, sergeant," I asked.

"You've already used up this much," he examined the tiny stump.

"I wrote a lot. But this time it came from my heart."

He left the door ajar, went to the guard room, or rather guard hole, and returned with a pencil. He knocked on my door twice that night. Once he asked if I ran out of paper. Then he came again when laughter shook me. I could not tell why I was laughing. Whether the Voice teased me with jokes, puns or memories, laughter descended upon me irresistibly, attacking me like a cramp.

The sergeant shook his head and confined his observations to opening the tiny steel window in the cell door. I heard him murmur: "They don't have a God, these people!"

I kept writing and writing without interruption. The Voice kept me on edge, saying again and again: it could make me laugh any minute.

In the morning, in the interrogation room, I tried so hard to suppress my laughter over the Voice's latest antics, I bit my lips until they bled. I pinched my thighs several times, even in front of "Sir". He must have noticed it because he kept eyeing me.

"Why have you been acting so strange the past few days?" he asked.

"Days?" I had been here only a couple of hours ago. True, a few meals interrupted the elapsed time, but it just couldn't have been days.

"The guard reported he saw you giggling for no reason at all and you scribbled all kinds of nonsense that did not interest us in the least."

He had not mentioned the poem. "I copied my underground poem for you, too," I bragged.

"What?"

"My poem, the one in which I attacked the Communist system."

"Did you spread it?"

"Yes."

"That won't help you much. Don't write similar nonsense in the future. Rather, write about your organization; that was a much weightier attack against the system. I warn you — you must behave!"

I did not understand his strong words. I had not given him any cause for the attack. Except when the Voice made me laugh, I followed all the rules.

I wrote what they wanted, then I wrote more. The guard took fistfulls of sheets from me. My hand cramped from writing, the lines became fuzzy in front of my eyes. I discussed every sentence twice with the Voice.

Despite all that, "Sir" accused me of keeping silent about important things and again warned me to behave.

"Write about anything that still bothers you deep inside!" were his parting words.

I gnawed the end of my pencil helplessly. What else could bother me? I had already resurrected all my innermost thoughts, examined and analyzed them.

Then, a new thought enthused me. I must analyze the conception of thoughts. I repeated to myself: "When the subconscious filters through conscience and becomes conscious, human thought is born."

I took the conclusion deduced with the help of the Voice and the Machine. I named the systematic methodology of the examination of conscience: "Investigative Principle." I chiseled into the paper: "The 'investigative principle' serves to bring to the surface the innermost secrets of the soul. They step out slowly, gradually, through rows of thoughts."

I stopped writing and looked at the text contentedly. The Voice threw water on my illusions: "What would a psychologist say about this? Dilettante work!"

The Voice was always right. I tried to contribute to the theory of the soulsearchers without any basic knowledge of psychology.

Two days had past... three?... or four?

My paper and pencil lay there untouched: I had nothing more to write.

The Voice relieved me, released me. Without the Voice I would turn into nothing. I knew if It did not defend me, they would kill me.

Last time "Sir" seemed much stiffer and more distrustful. He repeated his threats about "other methods." Why? What had I done against the system?

I could not make heads or tails out of the connection between Sir and the Voice. I found it impossible to believe the man knew about the Voice. He only made me write. Write! But, who ordered him to do so? Up to now, only the Voice had urged me to tell the truth. It led me to write, It stood behind my actions, It said I should believe the AVH.

And now, It disappeared again.

Or had It? Desperately, I listened to the silence.

Softly, like a hum when water starts boiling in the pot, or when they open a tap very quietly... a tiny sound buzzed in my ear. It was the Voice!

I strained my ears, cocked my head and stared at the arched ceiling of my death cell.

"Here I am!... Can you hear me?" Its friendly call beamed. The Voice came back in Its familiar strength, with decisive clarity: "You thought I had left you?" It mocked. "You could not explain a lot of things... you found Sir strange, the sergeant's rudeness shocked you. You saw him putting poison or medication in the soups."

The Voice's list missed my most important grievance: I found it extremely unjust that my honesty — in the service of truth — found no reward whatsoever.

"Do you really believe they want the truth?" It echoed the question I asked myself so often. "Can they be good people? Can they be part of me? Could you think, even for a minute, that I belonged with them?"

My confidence returned with the upsurge of blood flowing back into my limbs. I listened with excitement. The Voice's words, glorious in their revelation, resounded a long-awaited message; "NO, I NEVER BELONGED TO THEM!"

The moment's majesty took my breath: St. Paul must have turned towards the divine light with this kind of humble fright...

"Don't be afraid!" the Voice encouraged. "I led you, you believed me and followed my orders."

"I will be strong," I muttered.

"These are all enemies, you are in their prison. I am the only one who can follow you with the Machine. I can't do any more. I observe you and will tell the world."

"What about me?" my will to live burst into words.

"I will not let you perish. You will be needed as a witness."

I staggered in the light of this honor.

The clear definition of our roles made me happy, but I did not feel strong enough to continue. The present brought forth joy, but the future filled me with terror.

IN THE NAME OF THE SECRET SERVICE

Middle of November, 1952

"What would you say if tremendous changes had taken place on the outside? If I'd said that liberating troops swarmed the streets of Budapest?" the Voice announced one morning.

"Impossible!"

"Don't you think the world will some day have had enough of unilateral oppression?"

"It's possible."

"No one has heard of this underground cellar. They are looking for its entrance. You are the only one in contact with me. The few other prisoners kept here cannot imagine what is happening outside. You must tell them the news: Revolution! Uprising! Freedom!"

My breathing quickened. The Voice was getting me into trouble with Its inconceivable dreams. Had It revealed Its majesty for me to believe Its shocking news?

"You must do something!" It commanded. "Every minute is precious! Your life and those of others are at stake. You must act!"

"Me?"

"Yes. You. Will you do it?"

I took a deep breath. Frightened, I bit my lip: "I will."

"No matter what I command you to do?"

"I will do anything," I agreed, but I did not feel brave.

"Listen! Go to the door!... Right!... Now, bang at it with your fists and yell that you will take over the command of the AVH in the name of the secret service."

After a moment's hesitation, my screaming voice pierced the silence of our cellar-prison.

"In the name of the secret service... " I repeated, "I demand that the cells of the political prisoners be opened."

I obeyed, even though I had no idea whether the Voice dictated the truth, or what kind of "secret service" I was referring to? It could have been the 9 million suppressed Hungarians, the silent "secret service," all wanting truth, humanism and freedom.

Outside the guards nervously shuffled in their felt boots.

"I demand, in the name of the secret service... " I shouted, kicking the door. It opened vehemently as a lieutenant with a big scar and two sergeants grabbed me. The lieutenant covered my mouth with his hand.

"Come!" they pulled me out of my cell and up the stairs. I did not resist, merely listened attentively to the instructions of the Voice.

"Remember, the exit is at the end of the corridor. Past that — the street! Tear yourself away from them!" It ordered.

I slipped from the grip of my captors. I ran towards the gate and yelled at the frozen group of AVH men who had been loitering there: "I demand you open the gate, in the name of the secret service!"

The lieutenant and his accomplices caught up with me and wrestled me to the ground. They dragged me into a tiny room and twisted my arms to the back. The three of them could barely hold me. They wound a white sheet around my neck.

"See, they are careful," the Voice explained. "They don't dare choke you."

They bound me up fast following the lieutenant's instructions. I was not surprised. The Voice told me what would happen.

However, It failed to inform me about the newcomer: a civilian in a dark wintercoat, holding a black bag in his hand.

"Doctor!" I yelled at him.

His bulging eyes stared at me. He exchanged glances with the lieutenant. Finally he turned to me: "What makes you think I am a doctor?"[1]

"I know it! I have to caution you: I know everything that happens around me."

I stopped to wait for the Voice's prompting.

"I warn you. Don't you dare inject me with the serum to erase my ego!" I continued.

His bulge-eyes rolled from person to person around the room.

"Will you promise to behave like a normal human being?" he asked.

"Instruct them to take off my ties."

A miracle! Was it the magic of the Voice? Something frightened these people. Black-coat-bulge-eyes gave the lieutenant a signal to cut the string.

My limbs filled with tingling blood. Chills shook me. I kept my eyes on the newcomer's black bag that swung in his hand like a pendulum. It contained the injection: my death. My fate was in my own hands. I must let those people know they were in the midst of unusual events without betraying the Voice.

---

[1] I learned later, the doctor with the bulging eyes was Dr. Balint, a mental health specialist for the Communist concentration camps and the AVH. He went to Moscow in 1949 to study the methodology of medicinal processes. He was in charge of "psychiatric procedures," a specialist in torture.

"I have to warn you, Doctor, everything that transpires here is being recorded and filmed. You will have to answer for every one of your deeds in front of an international court."

Black-coat, whom I credited with being a doctor, looked questioningly at the lieutenant who was patiently winding the string.

"I will not give you the injection," he tried to quiet me, "but do behave properly."

"Why do you shut me off from the world?"

"Relax. You are a Christian... "

What did my relaxation have to do with Christianity?

"You must persuade them!" the Voice cut into the unusual association of ideas. "You must prove to them you can read human thoughts. I will help you!"

I straightened my back, trusting the Voice, and said unhesitatingly: "You think I don't know what happens outside? Not so long ago the Americans elected a new President. I could not communicate with anyone. Yet, I know his name." "Who is it?" the doctor asked curiously.

"You think I will name Stevenson," I followed the Voice's suggestion word-for-word. "You are mistaken; Mr. Eisenhower became President."

I was right; they did not say a word. I didn't need their confirmation. The Voice could not err. It would not weaken its power by being wrong.

"Understand, please, I know everything ahead of time. Everything that happens here will be on record and film."

Black-coat bit his lips and stiffly departed. They left me alone, **without any ties. I stayed quietly on the ground because I wanted to prove I had no intentions to disturb the peace.**

VISIONS?

Middle of November, 1952

I listened to the fantastic revelation of the Revolution with my face buried in my palms.

If we can see people's thoughts, if we have in our hands the extraordinary power of the Machine, we could well use it to further the cause of Hungarian freedom. We could switch the Machine's message on all the radio stations. The official announcers could talk as they wished, but people would hear only "our message." We would tell the whole world: Hungarians demand freedom. We would appeal to the Hungarian population to put out their flags. We'd demand the end of the power of the AVH. The country would ask for assurance of our freedom from the United Nations and the Western Powers. Hundreds of thousands would throng in the streets... hundreds of thousands in the celebration of freedom. With the help of the Machine, freedom would come without blood, without destruction.

I shook with exultation.

A new picture emerged: the Pope. I saw the radiant, tall figure of Pius XII, as I saw him in a private audience, twelve years ago, in 1940. He blessed me in the same room where Holy Pius X's deathbed stood. I found it reassuring to look up at this ascetic white apostle under the golden adornments created by Raffaello.

The Pope could call together a council. With the Machine, Christians would finally have to find unity. How could Buddhists, Moslims, Taoists believe in "one fold" if all the Christians of different denominations could not sort out their own faith? Why couldn't all the church officials from around the world meet? If the Pope called a council the Machine would undoubtedly be ready to serve him. Lies would disappear, every thought would be available to serve mankind.

Not even that would suffice. Everyone would be good! the Voice suggested. "Good — for the sake of being good. Think of Raffaello."

Raffaello Santi, the great artist of the Vatican stanzas, stood before me; so close, my hand could have touched his girlishly long curls.

I saw through him, into his empty workshop. The painter of the baby-faced Jesuses and beautiful Madonnas disappeared, or perhaps, stepped out for a moment.

"The workshop is not empty," the Voice joined me in my adventure, "look at his young apprentice."

The youth pulled out a small easel from the corner. He put a medium-sized picture on it and plunged his brush into the oilpaint. He worked on this picture only when the Master was gone. He prepared it in secret. A pink child, the child Jesus or maybe St. John the Baptist, played in the Raffaellish landscape. The round child-face glowed with worry-free mischief.

The young artist stepped back to examine the small masterpiece. He added some gray to the towering rocks of the background as if he felt their blue overpowered the composition. Contentedly he closed his eyes. Behind his eyelids he saw old Pietro come for the picture tomorrow. Who would know the Master had not created it?

He shuddered at the heavy touch on his shoulder. In his excitement he had not noticed the opening of the door and the entrant, Raffaello, whose hand now rested on his shoulder.

"Your picture is beautiful; I could have painted it myself!" the Master said looking deep into the eyes of the lobster-red apprentice. "Why did you keep it secret? Pietro buys it from you for a good price? Wait! You can get much more for it if we sell it as my picture."

He sat down in front of the painting and, in his usual sunny mood that brightened everyone's day, he finished the masterpiece.

"Now you will get a good price for it!"

"Do you think this vision was true?" the Voice asked, bringing me back to my prison cell.

I left the question unanswered. I had no idea where reality ended and the dreamlike narcosis began, where I started living the episodes. If the Machine filmed all of these conscious or half-conscious technicolor visions, then it would become self-evident which was imagination and which the gray reality.

I waited impatiently, with a feverish excitement for the next adventure. Ignoring the grim cell around me, I understood. I had to scrutinize the stories of history's immortals in order to learn from their fates. I had to search for the good in their actions and analyze their mistakes.

In the blink of an eye, I went from the king of renaissance painting to the great renaissance King of Hungary, Matthias Corvin.[1]

The majestic ruler, chosen by his people, wore laurels woven of folk-legends, all depicting his goodness. Yet, even he: where did this infinitely good king fail?

Close to me now, I saw him who conquered Vienna; the son of the great Hunyadi, hero of Hungary's fights against the Turks. He did not

---

[1] Matthias (Corvin) Hunyadi (1440-1490) was one of the greatest Hungarian kings. He excelled as commander, lawmaker, patron of renaissance arts and sciences, and as the founder of the first permanent Hungarian army (Black Army). His early death prevented him from putting a definitive end to the Turkish offensive against Europe.

appear as customarily portrayed by flattering sculptors, riding high on his horse, in his full royal splendor. He knelt, crouching in his pew, tortured by gout, struggling with his own thoughts.

"Where did I go wrong? I didn't heed the warnings of my conscience. I turned my anger against the Austrian emperor because of his envy, pride, indifference. I fought him because I wanted to assure a sturdy ally at my back when attacking Islam. Did I move too hastily? Maybe I should not have humbled Vienna. My pride ran away with me. I forgot: I too was mortal. I wasted Hungarian blood against Christians. I was no good, only foolishly brave!"

The king bent his head onto his arms. His long, brown hair cascaded over his gout-tortured body: "I was amiss! I omitted much good I could have done," I heard him whisper. His voice still echoed in me when the royal apparition disappeared.

"Taps," (or was it "reveille?") startled me. I could not remember my last meal. Food didn't interest me. I didn't touch it. The exciting adventures, emerging one after another behind my closed eyelids, held my hunger. My attention returned to present day Hungarian freedom. I wanted to find out whether the system had indeed changed drastically, whether freedom had opened its flag; and, if so, whether I would ever be free. Would they let me out to join the celebrating crowd?

The Voice cooled my enthusiasm. "They'll never find you unless you give them a signal. They won't even know you existed. You must give them a sign that you are alive," It continued, leading me back to reality. "Start with your name. Now you no longer pretend to be crazy. You fight for your life. Hurry, I command you!"

I shouted my name and protested being kept in secret. Guarded whispering, shuffling, the opening of a door, and soft talk were my only answers.

"Political prisoners... I am Tottosy... Our time to act... " The lieutenant with the big scar and the two sergeants wrestled me to the cot. They tied my feet together with a thin string. They fastened them to the cot. They tied my hands, already held together by handcuffs. They pulled my tied hands to my feet, bending my spine in two. The handcuffs plowed a bloody furrow into my wrists. Sweat poured down my face. I felt like a galley slave. My torturer's sweat dripped.

"So! Think twice before you yell. If you as much as open your mouth... "

I closed my eyes. They went out, leaving the door ajar. With the little strength I had left, I tried to satisfy the Voice.

"Fellow prisoners," I groaned, "I am Tottosy, still alive!... "

The two sergeants immediately appeared. The rude-faced older one and a pointy-chinned younger one. The younger one pushed a dirty, wet rag into my mouth. It burned like hell. The older one tied a black "gagger" over the rag. He tightened the rags so well, I could get no sound out. I wanted to scream. I hurt terribly. Only my self-confidence stopped me and last, but not least, the "gagger." My hands puffed up on both sides of the strings, as did my head and feet.

The Voice assured me with bitter logic. If they so strenuously suppressed the broadcast of my name, then obviously this was bad for them and good for me.

The young sergeant paused in front of me, with hatred, typical of idiots, written all over his face. He could not be touched by any human emotion, especially weakness. How he would scream in my place! I felt myself stronger than he was, even in the midst of torture; my entire face bathed in sweat, tears pouring from my eyes. He held a huge key-ring in his hand, rattling the mass of keys. He couldn't stop his self-induced hate and struck me hard with his key-ring. Blood flooded my nose. I couldn't breathe through my mouth, so I desperately groped for air, then finally groaned. With every movement the handcuffs cut deeper into my flesh.

The guy with the keys brought another black "gagger." He meaningfully placed the rag onto the cot in front of me. His action talked louder than words: if he applied that rag to my nose I was finished. I would slowly choke. I knew he would do it, too.

Without turning my head, the fragments of words scribbled onto the wall, the tiny crosses, the good-bye words, the brown bloodspots displayed themselves in front of my eyes. I imagined the long row of tortured people, while I gazed at the last messages of those who would never see sunlight again.

I wondered about who had preceded me in this cell: was Cardinal Mindszenty among them? Again his wide-open drugged eyes appeared before me, as I saw them during his trial. They seemed to be wandering in an unknown land. Maybe my cell was the very spot where they had murdered Bishop Meszleny or where Attorney General Ries' life had been taken.

I prayed the young sergeant wouldn't come back to tie that other **rag over my nose! On the other hand: death might bring relief.** I guessed that two hours had passed since they had started this torture, but it could have been three... or four.

The young sergeant returned, but he did not reach for the rag. He satisfied himself by dealing me another blow to my head with his key-ring.

"Old bastard!"

Old? Have I aged so much in the past few months? Fear paralyzed me with the picture of him lifting that rag after and tying it around my nose. Already I strained for air with one of my nostrils blocked by a dried blood cot. I didn't dare moan because the young one might shush me with more than his threatening whisper: "Can't you be quiet?"

I was relieved when he left. How could these tortures lead to life? Maybe the Voice will not be able to prevent my death in this dirty hole after all, only my fate will be shown to the world through films and tapes. How much proof does this insane world need? Every day, every month brought its own proofs and yet, no one really believed it. It was, oh, so much simpler not to believe the bloody present, or to simply turn away from the sight of a crushed human wreck. I longed to lose consciousness.

The "gagger" and the scribbled hieroglyphs on the wall painted a dark future. My bladder was bursting... I could no longer hold it.

Thirty-three years! Old age! Maybe it was the eighth of December today, my thirty-third birthday.

I prayed and listened to the buzzing consolation of the Voice. My face twitched, my body puffed up, burned, like the liquid that at ate at my mouth. Finally unconsciousness saved me from pain.

At reveille, when the mess-tins arrived, I came to my senses with my limbs still tied, swollen to the size of pillows. The spitting sergeant was on duty again. He hurried to cut off my strings. I patted the white pillows of my arms and my feet the way a beast licks his wounds.

I had spent more than eight hours tied hand and foot.

Yesterday, I could not eat anything and this morning the Voice forbade me to eat my breakfast: "Watch what you eat! They will poison you. Don't touch the food!" Yesterday the beautiful visions made me forget food, but today hunger hurt. Yet, I obeyed and returned my mess-tin without touching it.

Slowly the morning brought new spirit. Blood flowed again into my puffed up limbs. I survived! I made my signal! New spiritual adventures beckoned. A new magic enveloped me: peace.

Peace, humanity's age-old, deepest desire, will crown love, truth and freedom. God wants love. The Creator will punish everyone who does not search for peace.

A new vision emerged.

We walked on the fields of Mohacs. On the hillside, framed by a forest, armies prepared for the fight. I clearly saw the Hungarian riders in their glistening armors, their carriages, the messengers' horses, and, a bit father away, the young king surrounded by his commanders.[2]

In the sultan's camp the big cannons were well hidden by bushes. Soliman, the sultan, prayed in his ornate tent behind the cannons. He called up his messengers: "Watch carefully," he said to them. "When

---

[2]The battle of Mohacs: August, 1526.

the lances point to the sun, the offensive of the janichars will change direction. They will start a false retreat to the South."

The sultan mounted his white horse. The battle raged. Blood spilled onto the grass. Moaning, cries to Allah and supplications to Christ mingled in the air. The sultan watched stiffly. His chief messenger with the lance waited for the sultan's order. The messenger raised his Tartar-like face in ecstasy to his commander, watching for the signal from the Father of Islam. Finally the sultan's lips moved. The messenger immediately executed the order: "Hold your lance towards sunrise!"

The Turkish army retreated. As they ran to the sunrise, behind them followed the glistening Hungarians, drunk with their glory, dreaming about victory... They followed... Running to their deaths! The lance moved again and suddenly the spahi equestrian forces parted. The cannons, hidden behind the bushes, showered abundant death onto the unsuspecting troops.

I saw the fleeing young Hungarian king's horse slide on the slimy stones of a creek. This stream became the deathbed of both the archbishop and the king — representing the faith and the power of the country.

The vision broke. Another one took its place: Byzantium, crushed by the Turks. Soloman, the sultan, knelt on a prayer carpet after the victory in his huge hall covered with expensive silks and carpets.

Outside the divan[3] hummed, but the sultan was talking with Allah. He harbored doubts in his heart: he did not serve a good cause at Mohacs.

He debated whether death was Allah's true will for the young king. Or should he, the sultan, have tried for a peaceful settlement? Can true peace emerge from battlefields emitting moans of the dying and deadly plague?

"I want no more wars!" the sultan declared in the divan. The janichars groaned in astonishment.

"Is he out of his mind?" they whispered. "He lets the results of a victorious battle go down the drain. We must crush the infidels! We will force him to fight!"

The vision disappeared.

"Is it possible," the Voice inquired, "that Solomon was overcome with doubts? He didn't use the advantages of a victorious battle. Why? Maybe he wanted to gain new strength and more time to attack Buda. Was everything you just saw possible?

"Why don't you eat your lunch?" the guard roused me.

"They want to poison me."

"Don't be stupid."

[3]Divan: council of the sultan.

"What did they put in my soup?"

He shut the door without answering.

"Where are the liberators?" My thoughts turned back to the revolt in Budapest, allegedly regaining its freedom. The Voice kept warning me about the danger of the outsiders not being able to find the door to this secret poison. If we could not connect with the outside world, my situation was hopeless. It seemed highly unlikely that the spitting sergeant would enlighten someone of our whereabouts.

I knew I had to give another sign of life. Yet, I shrunk from the prospects of another night's tortures. I debated, but the Voice's will and my life instinct won. The guards did not like my signal, so it had to be good for me. I simply had to do it!

I yelled my name as loud as I could. The lieutenant and the two sergeants were faster today than yesterday. They easily overpowered me, although I saw, the spitting sergeant did not like his job.

In a few minutes I was back in the galley slave position, tied up like a ham, in full pain. This time, they did not saturate the rag with the burning liquid, they did not bring in the black gagger and no-one beat me with the key-ring.

I learned that different levels of torture existed; mostly it depended on the torturer. My hands and feet puffed up to pillows again, but unconsciousness embraced me only shortly before breakfast-time.

I didn't eat that day either. I poured the soup under the cot, according to the orders from the Voice. The spitting one noticed it, but he left me alone. He just shook his head and gruffed at me, denouncing my craziness.

Was the Voice's suggestion, a few hours later, part of this craziness? I distinctly heard It proclaim the AVH would kill me in my cell. Why would It say anything untrue?

The inhabitants of the other cells had not said one word so far. I only knew about them because I heard the daily noise of the mess-tins as they were handed to the prisoners. There couldn't be any more than four or five people, who kept as silent as ghosts. I, on the other hand, gave signs of life. I caused trouble, disturbed their "order." Why shouldn't they render me harmless? I knew they instructed the guard to kill me in my cell — with a dagger. They would wait till the spitting one went home. Or maybe they had asked him to do it exactly because I seemed to trust him.

I could not idly wait for this to happen: I had to do something.

"Sergeant!" I whispered through the bars above the door. "I know you received an order to kill me, but I also know you won't do it!"

If I told him to his face that he couldn't possibly kill me, maybe he wouldn't actually do it.

He opened the door and asked: "What did you say?"

"I know they want to kill me, but you won't do it, because deep down you are a good man."

He didn't say a word, just looked at me, groping for an answer.

"Let's shake on it that you won't murder me. I trust you!" I said, offering my hand.

We shook hands. He didn't say anything, not even when he locked the door again.

I felt more peaceful. My frights vanished with the appearance of a new vision. Dante visited me, the stern giant of La Divina Comedia, the immortal emigrant, who dreamed about the ecstasies and the punishments of the nether world, bringing them to life through his poetry. Why did I see him? Maybe because he lived in a separate world, looked for the blueprint of his dream Heaven. According to him, we all receive only as much of Heaven as we deserve. People will be punished only to the extent to which their intellects understood the sins they committed.

Why couldn't God prepare a Dante-like Heaven for Dante? I felt the grim look of the Florentian mystic upon me. I heard the scraping of his goose-feather on the pergamon as he added new lines to his work. Only he could hear God's voice from infinity: "I will create for you the kind of Heaven you dreamed for yourself."

Is Hell within us? Does Heaven grow from our innermost beings? We forget God when we are happy. A sad fate often separates us from Him. I realized I hadn't truly prayed for days.

Disregarding the frequent twisting of the peep-hole I began my prayer. I sensed that the spitting one watched me from the outside. I prayed kneeling; it strengthened my confidence. I had to show there was something much stronger than fright. My knees started to throb; I stopped. The Voice accused me of faithlessness.

I started over.

The door opened and a mess-tin banged on the floor. The guard stopped for a few seconds, probably watching me, then I remained alone with my dish. I hadn't touched food for three days, but I didn't dare to get up without having said at least one prayer all the way to the end. I repeated stubbornly: "I believe in one God..."

I began again.

Morning found me on the cot, kneeling, deep in my thoughts, awake, but at least I had escaped one night of torture.

CRIES INTO NOTHINGNESS

End of November, 1952

Six out of ten days I suffered being hog-tied. Whenever I cried my name, morning or night, the torture began and lasted until the next morning. This procedure slowly developed into a routine.

In the room of the goat-faced "Sir," they tied me to my chair, just as Indians tied up their victims before scalping them. When even "Sir's" compassionless face reflected shock, I wondered if this was a new method for the AVH.

"What did you do this time?" he complained. "I told you to behave."

"I only yelled out my name."

"That goes against our rules."

"I want to give a sign of life. Great changes are taking place on the outside."

"You don't say. What kind of changes?"

The Voice did not permit me to answer. They would kill me if I talked about the power of the Machine, the role of the radios, the Hungarian revolution, the resurrection of freedom.

"Untie him!" the interrogator ordered the rude-faced sergeant.

"Now," the Voice said. "The time has come to let the AVH know about your special talent."

I wanted to shock "Sir," to show him I could read his thoughts.

"Have you read the 'Novel of the Next Century'?" I asked daringly.

"What?" his mouth twitched.

"The novel by Jokai, about the next century!"

He didn't answer.

"Don't you think, Sir, that with today's advanced technology we should be able to guess other people's thoughts?"

"What an idea!"

"Let's try!" I suggested.

"Sir" smiled with the expression of someone who just bit into a lemon.

"Like a goat grazing on wet grass," the Voice mocked.

"Lieutenant, you are now thinking about... " I waited for the Voice to fill me in on the details, "what color tie you wore last."

I watched his expression, although I knew his opinion would not make any difference. The Voice could not err.

"And now you are thinking of what your answer should be to the offer you received for a trip to Moscow. You cannot let them know you are afraid of being kept there. You are looking for an alibi not to go..."

He didn't protest... he didn't laugh... he didn't deny it...

He waved to the guard who had just stepped in on cue to take me back to my cell.

They did not tie me up that day. The Voice kept me from eating. For the past eight days the Voice had given me permission to eat only occasionally, and never more than a few crumbs. Hunger was a cruel cell-mate, it didn't listen to arguments. The red-colored paprika sauce, handed in by the guards, started my gastric acids flowing. I argued with the Voice. Finally it allowed me to taste the soup. I gobbled it up as fast as I could, but too soon the Voice stopped me, reminding me to exercise self-discipline. It condoned my breaking off a piece of the bread and devouring it, along with half my food. No more; only half of it — after eight days.

At least my cell was warm and I did not freeze as in my cell at Veszprem. The stuffy air pressed heavily on my worn body. My coat was torn as a result of my struggles with the guards. My ragged pants smelled of urine, but then, animals get used to their own smell. These discomforts became meaningless compared to the new dangers the Voice uncovered.

"Can they flood the cells with gas?" It threatened.

"Maybe," I answered, beginning to smell something suspicious.

"Hurry," It urged.

I only had to take one step to reach the door. My cry broke the silence. "Political prisoners, it is I, Tottosy! Listen, they want to poison us with gas!"

The routine consequences followed.

When I regained consciousness in the morning, I felt content: the Voice prevented them from poisoning us with gas.

I patted my puffed up face and pricked up my ears. I could detect the guards approaching, even when they wore their felt boots.

I found it especially eerie that none of my prison-mates ever made a sound, or gave signs of life. I could hear the termites gnawing at the building, but from the other human beings no sound came — ever. They asked nothing from their wardens, no signs or groans broke the silence of the prison. Their presence became evident merely through the occasional squeaking of the doors and the clinking of the mess-tins as the guards placed them on the floor. My ghost-mates, paralyzed by fear, by that dreaded discipline so often mentioned by "Sir," kept their constant silence. Recently I had not even heard their mess-tins. Did our keepers drug them into a stupor or kill them?

Suddenly I heard an odd noise, as if clothes swished around in the corridor. It sounded like many guards walking around, wrapping the bodies of my silent prison-mates into sheets and dragging them out of their cells.

I wondered if the cadavers now lay on the red matting of the corridor. Will they burn them, or throw them into the sewer? For those unfortunates it no longer mattered that all of this would be preserved by the Machine for future generations. A good feeling crept over me: the Machine would protect me. It compelled me to protect my own life. I could not remain silent, or pretend I was dead, too.

"Political prisoners... " I screamed my usual sentence.

The usual ensemble answered my call. This time they dragged me through the empty corridor, down to the gate that led to the exit. At the end of the worn matting they opened a tiny iron door. It led to a small hole, no bugger than a doghouse. They tried to push me into this hole. I resisted with superhuman strength. Finally, the three iron-fisted young men managed to squeeze me in. The Voice's scream cut into my brain: "Don't let yourself be locked into that concrete cell! If they manage to close the door, you will suffocate."

My feet were still outside. I latched one foot in the opening and braced myself on the concrete walls. That saved me. No matter how much they beat, pinched and kicked my foot, I was determined: even if only a stub remained, I would not budge from my position.

In the end they tired and gave up.

I kicked open the iron door with a renewed surge of strength. I didn't climb out. I was afraid they were trying to trick me. I could see the sparks in their eyes and the sweat on their brows. The lieutenant wiped his face with a blue-edged handkerchief. His scar was blood-red and looked ready to burst. He gasped: "Promise, you'll never shout anymore!"

"Promise you will take me to the prosecutor!" I retorted.

They looked at each other helplessly.

I climbed out from the concrete doghouse. They stepped behind me, but they didn't lift a finger. They let me stagger back to my cell and even left the door open for a few minutes. They must have expected me to start yelling again.

I stayed alive... because I listened to the Voice.

* * *

I thought of a million tricks to get in contact with the outside world. First I knocked for the lieutenant and demanded to speak with Rakosi, the leader of the Communist Party.[1] He didn't show any signs of shock and quietly listened while I argued that I had to warn Comrade Rakosi about a revolution ready to break out any minute. Today he could still escape and prevent bloodshed. I had no idea what he should have done. The audience merely served as a good alibi to get out of prison: the Voice inspired me to this daring demand. I wanted out of this death-cell to testify in front of a prosecutor, a judge, the people.

It didn't come as a surprise that he gave no sign of taking me seriously. My terrified cries amounted to nothing more than danger signals of helplessness and despair. Cries in the wilderness, searching for a legal solution to my problem.

Why would Rakosi believe me, a worn, tortured political prisoner? Why would this conceited, professional revolutionary believe that his empire, too, could fall. He was standing on sand with no bonding material. Sand was not stone or cement, only a softly oozing mass of a billion tiny granules, which, when well shaken, would take the shape of any dish, would fill in every crevice, but would never, never be capable of bonding anything.

No flower grew in the sand, yet sand could cover a giant if he fell in it. Rakosi was not a person who would ever admit to standing on sand. I had to try another idea. No matter what, I wanted out of this pit.

I knocked again. Even if my efforts resulted in nothing, the Machine would record every try. The lieutenant showed patience to my second demand which he knew he was not going to fulfill.

Not even his scar twitched when I offered a goodly sum of dollars to the AVH if they took me to a notary public and there promised to adhere to the law, even with my person.

I presented my case slowly, the lieutenant nodded: "I will report it."

I sensed he wanted to get rid of me but was obliged to playact for the benefit of the two guards who had accompanied me to him. My unilateral dialogue resembled the galley slave's bargaining with his master.

I almost fell over a huge steaming kettle in the middle of the room. The bubbling water seemed like the modern version of a witch's brew spiced with frogs and snakes. It terrified me, though it may well have been the lieutenant's washwater.

---

[1]Matthias Rakosi was Party Secretary of the Hungarian Communist Party (later renamed the Hungarian Workers' Party) from 1945 to July of 1956. He was also the Chairman of the Council of Ministers in 1952.

By that time, I no longer felt the need to wash. The order to shave the following day was entirely unexpected. The evil-faced sergeant took me upstairs. I couldn't help thinking: shaving would be a good occasion for them to cut my throat, using my madness as an alibi. The loudspeaker of Veszprem had warned me about that kind of possible "chicken-death." It could well become reality now. I forced myself to relax and — the shaving passed without incident.

While going down the stairs, back to my cell, the Voice suggested I push the sergeant down the stairs. He hurried in front of me and my hands were not tied. Should I gather my strength and give him a great heave? He'd tumble down the steps and might break his neck.

An inner brake stopped me: I couldn't do it! I had no right to acquire freedom at the expense of another's life. I had no right to sacrifice blood in order to stop my own bleeding. I had to walk in the ways of truth. The only possibility open for me was defense.

The Voice brought another terrifying thought that night: authorities plan to murder me with mustard gas.

My usual cries were followed by the usual punishment. I had to evoke the galley slave torture again and again because I had to obey the life-saving Voice.

Later, the spitting sergeant untied my strings, then led me into a mystifying place. The room looked like an alchemist's lab in the Middle Ages. All around us on the walls I saw test-tubes, reports, and medicinal jars. Only the desk was modern. A medical doctor sat in front of me. On his uniform he wore the golden epaulet of a lieutenant colonel.

He turned a bright lamp on me and examined my eye reflexes. He didn't ask anything, but waved his dismissal to the guard who led me back to my cell.

Sleepy tiredness crept over me. Strong shocks, like those emitted by electricity, occasionally passed through my body.

I wanted to sleep but the voice did not let me. It tried to persuade me that the medical exam was the forerunner of the injection. If I proved unable to give a definitive sign of life, sooner or later they would give me the shot to make me lose my self-identity forever. That terrified me.

I ate my lunch bitterly. I found a strong taste in my bread. The Voice confirmed my suspicion: they tried to poison us with arsenic. **Unwillingly I fulfilled my newest task, namely to alert the other prisoners with the help of my cries.**

"Prison-mates... " as soon as I finished the introductory words, four of the guards fell on me and pushed me into the alchemist's room where now another medical lieutenant colonel sat at the table. He looked Spanish. He held a syringe in his hand.

The end was here! They were now going to paralyze my will.

"I protest!" I screamed. "I protest against this injection!"

His face was indifferent as he got up. The syringe flashed in his hand.

"This will only make you sleep!"

They held me tight, I stood there, unable to defend myself.

As they took me down the stairs, I felt my strength dwindle. The spitting one brought more blankets and put them down beside me on the cot. Did he want them handy to wrap my cadaver?

I became more melancholy, my limbs turned numb: this was death. My eyes fell on the sheets of paper I hadn't used for weeks. It had been quite a while since I last wrote my confessions, my self-accusations. I pulled out one of the papers. I propped my elbow onto the pile of blankets and, holding the pencil in my fist, started to write in big, slanted letters:

"I REVOKE ALL MY CONFESSIONS! GOD BE WITH YOU! DEATH TO THE MURDERERS!"

With my last strength I draped the paper on the other cot. Then numbness came over my being and in the next instant I felt nothing at all...

THE DARING DECLARATION

Beginning of December, 1952

Several gold-epauleted officers stood in the cell door. I saw their fuzzy outlines the way a drunk man sees. According to rules I should stand: I tried with all my might — in vain. I plunged back onto the cot. My strength would not reach as far as climbing on all fours.

Were they asking me something? or just talking to one another? Had I understood their question, I still could not have forced my stuttering, stammering mouth to form words in answer to their inquiries.

The gold shoulder marks flashed once more, then I fell back into unconsciousness.

Hours, or even days had passed... I couldn't tell if my life depended on it. I woke slowly. One by one my searching eyes recognized, then made sense of the objects in my moldy, bleak surroundings. The blinding lightbulb proved to me I still lived. I sat up. They had not killed me after all, only knocked me out.

The piece of paper! Where was it? It no longer lay on the cot where I had left it. They had received my message. What good did it do? Nobody on the outside knew I was still among the living and I was kept in this hole.

How could I give a better sign of life? I remembered the corridor's tiny, impenetrably dirty window as a possibility. Another one would be the window in the interrogation room — that might work.

When I found myself alone with the goat-chinned interrogator in that ominous room, I jumped to the window to pull up the shades. He leaped up as fast as I had and we struggled hard. He must have pushed the danger button because guards immediately entered and tied me to my chair before they left me alone again with the goat-chinned one. He took out a revolver from the desk drawer.

"I could shoot you now," he said, aiming the pistol at me. "No one would question it, if I said you attacked me during the interrogation. If you behave like that once more I'll send you to the netherworld."

His threat did not affect me.

"What did you want with the window?" he asked while he shut the gun in the drawer.

"I wanted to shout."

"Why?"

"You have kept me here illegally for months. When will you try me in front of a judge?"

"WE CAN SETTLE YOUR CASE IN OUR OWN JURISDICTION!"

Cold sweat broke out on my brow. I first heard this sentence when I asked the state prosecutor about one of my clients in 1951. He said "I can tell you nothing. The AVH has his file. They will settle the case in their own jurisdiction." The cold sweat broke out on my brow at that time, as it did now, only this time the words applied to me.

The Voice was my only consolation. Without It, my life would have been a total loss. On the other hand, what kind of life was this, underground, like a mole? What would I do without my visions and dreams? The Voice's magic provided me with an escape from threatening reality. In Its company I no longer suffered the miseries of prison, the noises of the stifled sighs, the clinking keys, the opening food-windows and peep-holes. Liberated, I flew to another planet where only the Voice could follow me. That was life's meaning for me at the moment.

The slowly rising fog brought the majestic vision of a stately, proud human figure, mounted on his horse. The vision showed him exactly the way I had admired him countless times in course of my childhood, in the center of the big millennial monument. His noble figure seemed lonely now, riding the wild mountain trails.

Why did the Chieftain of the prairies ride into the mountains? He urged his horse to gallop; ignoring the gaping ravines. A waterfall interrupted the natural trail. The white horse reared back, as if frightened by the sudden vision. Beyond the mountain ridge the blinding blue-glimmer of the Adriatic Sea appeared in its full splendor.

The rider immersed himself in the beauty of infinity embracing the azur of the sea. The horse's nostrils emitted a warm cloud of vapor as he pranced. He galloped towards the water, his mouth foaming. His rider couldn't stop him. The waves broke high onto the shore. Their bottomless blueness swallowed horse and rider.

I shook my head in confusion. Arpad had never reached the Adriatic Sea. A later tribal leader, referred to in a document at a convent in Dalmatia, a Pagan Magyar chieftain rode his horse into the sea. His name, the details were never recorded. Why had the Voice confused me?

I stretched my mind way back, in order to reach Arpad. Some black fate haunted the Chieftain's family. Some of its members were born with six fingers, others suffered from hemophilia. They led their troops into battle with the certain knowledge they would die from even the smallest of wounds. The Pagan Hungarians sent robbing expeditions into the West, presenting a terrible menace to Europe. Then, as Christians, they became the bastions of Western civilization. tion.

Majesty, power, bravery and tragedy all received their role in the royal family of Arpad. I recalled Saman, the Pagan priest, and the curse he cast on Arpad and his family, for having taken on the meek, benevolent God of the Christians, in place of the War-god of old. Was it the effect of this curse that haunted the royal family?

I approached these questions with awe. Who conjectured these pictures onto the monitor of my brain? My detailed studies of history, the traditions of my family and the tiny unknown particles in my blood — they all could have played a role in my visions.

Ancient Hungarian texts crowded my mind and I heard a resounding voice solemnly address me: "arpad the Chieftain stands before you. He looks onto you, son of his blood. He returns now to resurrect the spirit of the ancestors. Roused from the dead as the wind rises on mountaintops, he speeds into the valley, to you, to you."

I knew I had to answer this message in the same rhythm of language in which it addressed me. I called to whoever sent this warning in the way of our ancestors.

"Whoever you are, the suffering humble search for your outstretched hand. Wherever your shining spirit dwells, it reaches us across the millenium. Our silent respect pays homage to you, Arpad, our great Chieftain. We are the continuation of your blood, the stream of your soul, the echoes of your voice. Life does not cease, it merely changes forms. You stand before us now, on the mountain, or on the prairie, in front of an altar, or on horseback. This way you live with us and in us, like the seed that sprouts into a blossom, then blooms to ripen into seed again in order to carry on the essence of the race."

A strange ecstasy prompted my improvisation. The Voice ripened the words in me, whether they sounded good, bad, beautiful or uncouth. To me they exemplified unintelligible beauty.

This dream went beyond earlier ones meant to explain certain issues through the lives of immortals like Raffaello, Dante, and Matthias Corvin. This one had a special purpose.

The words implied my genes continued in the age-old bloodline and tradition of Arpad, the Chieftain. The Voice wanted to persuade me I was a tiny granule of quartz from the golden-shined nugget which started with Arpad and led to my cell. It argued the unstoppable continuity, human eternity. Its thesis seemed impossible at first; yet the more It argued, the more I believed. I remembered a genealogist in our family who had harbored similar ideas. Could it be true? Dizziness overtook me at the thought of it. Memory took me back to the days when I was a student watching the waves break on the seashore, sprinkling their salty froth towards me, while I stood for hours on the Dalmatian beach, observing their ever-changing spectacle. The vision of an ancient chief disappearing in the foams of the

Adriatic Sea united me with Arpad. His horse rode into the sea with him, but his spirit merged with mine and continued to live in the youngster watching the waves.

The chronicles contained nothing about my ancestry's exact relations to Arpad. But the Voice confidently emphasized that beyond the gaping written records, there existed a more mysterious and greater proof: the Voice's soulsearching power. It penetrated the mysteries of the genes and discovered truth.

"You are the continuation of the Arpad family!" It repeated.

My soberness rejected this nonsense. It would constitute a grave error to believe in an improvable dream, a supposition.

"I will prove it, me, the Voice!" I heard It question and repeat Its arguments. It struggled against my stubbornness and urged me to concede.

Finally I realized: the Voice must have known something about me, or why would It have chosen me, of all the people, to protect me from death, from the AVH's cellar. There were others more worthy, others who had suffered more. Yet I continued to resist. Why couldn't I be the chosen survivor, the one to carry on the blood of my famous ancestor?

The Voice's siege exhausted me more from obedience to the Voice than conviction. I conceded to be Arpad's descendant. I believed in the resurrecting instinct of the genes, in the Voice's total ability to see and hear everything.

I realized my choice: I would either have to trust the Voice completely, or entirely reject It. However, if I decided to believe in It, I took on the responsibility of the name. I had to let the world know. I started to yell: "I AM A DIRECT DESCENDANT OF THE HOUSE OF ARPAD."

* * *

"Why are you yelling?" the spitting sergeant asked. "Who do you think you are?"

"I am a descendant of Arpad," my voice shook as I answered.

He banged the door wide open.

Naturally, I felt privileged to come from the House of Arpad, but simultaneously I began to realize: this recognition had not increased my chances of survival — to the contrary.

If I thought my ancestry might impress the guards into staying away from me, I was sorely mistaken. My wrists, badly wounded from earlier times, were tied even tighter, but I just gnashed my teeth. This time fainting was more merciful and saved me from my pains sooner than ordinarily.

The spitting one removed my strings and took me to the Spanish-faced doctor.

"You will receive a sedative!" the lieutenant colonel informed me.

"I don't want it!"

"Then the guards will hold you down!"

"I protest against the altering of my consciousness!"

"Hold out your hip!" he commanded and pushed the needle into my flesh.

In my cell I pulled the cover over my head and sank into a narcotic slumber.

That afternoon "Sir" again complained about my behavior.

"Not only do you yell all kinds of nonsense, you also incite a revolutionary mood among the inmates," he said raising his voice. "We have strict punishments against inciting."

"To stand up for my rights is not inciting. Take me to the prison hospital if I am sick, or to the prosecutor if I am healthy!"

He kept his silence. He knew criminal law as well as I did. He knew no investigation could last beyond six months without the involvement of the prosecutor.

"I can't stand it any more, lieutenant!" I blurted out in despair.

"I told you not to call me 'lieutenant.' Besides, where do you get this idea of my being a 'lieutenant'?"

I could not betray the Voice, but I stubbornly kept calling him "lieutenant" from then on. If he did not like it, then it had to be good for me.

"Please take me away from here," I begged.

"I will try to arrange it," he answered.

I couldn't believe it. A few hours later two AVH officers came to my cell. A few minutes, several iron gates and a narrow door later we stepped onto a street of Budapest. I couldn't register any of the pedestrians' faces because the officers pushed me quickly into an elegant passenger car waiting for us at the door. A submachine-gun carrying AVH sat beside the chauffeur. The evil-faced AVH, the third one in uniform, crowded into the front seat. I squeezed between two civilians in the back.

They pulled the car's curtains, but through the slits I could peek at the streets of the capital. To my disappointment, I saw no sign of change, disquiet, or revolution whatsoever.

Indifferent pedestrians waited for streetcars, carefully avoiding the white remnants of snow and pools of mud. It must have been sometime in December, 1952. I had not carved a calendar onto the wall with my nails since the Voice supplied me with what information I needed.

A brown-haired woman in a fur coat crossed in front of our car. She held a small net shopping bag. Further down the street we stopped for a red light. Through the windshield the swarming of the tumultuous streets of Budapest lured me: there... there was freedom!

The Voice's questions could not distract my foreboding: they were taking me to my death.

I saw no recognizable landmarks. Pedestrians became scarce, traffic died down, the car wobbled on cobblestones. The driver shifted into high gear and we sped ahead.

We arrived at the foot of a high wall of what looked like a castle with tall watchtowers. AVH guards with submachine guns manned the towers. Only a miracle would keep me from being taken into this building.

"Pray!" the Voice prodded.

I couldn't pray, only broken supplications left my lips. I was afraid they'd treat me with electric shocks here, or maybe they'd cremate me. My escorts must have thought of me as being a dangerous madman. I desperately wanted to avert entering this prison.

As a last resort I declared: "You are taking the last prince of the House of Arpad."

They showed no sign of comprehending what I said: no warning, no hushing, no mockery, no surprise — nothing.

The car stopped in front of the main gate of the castle. It opened slowly, two AVH men pulling wide the wings of the gate. We drove into a small courtyard, blocked by another gate closing off the road in front of us. The first gate locked behind us and we were stuck in the tiny courtyard between the two.

The evil-faced sergeant and the civilian AVH on my right got out. The other AVH, still sitting next to me, squeezed my hand harder. He worried in vain. I had no intentions of jumping out of the car. Where could I have run between the two gates?

I showered desperate questions onto the Voice. I wanted to know where I was and what was happening to me. A million bees buzzed in my head, but I did not show my deadly fear that made me stare at the mysterious second door. My entourage carefully observed the formalities. My nerves made me shake all over.

"God, please, just don't let that second door open."

Why should my supplications be heard? One wasn't taken on rides like this without a well thought-out plan, a command.

Hours — or was it minutes? — passed.

The second gate opened wide enough to let the evil-faced one and the AVH man get through the slit. Now... now... they would make me walk through that door.

They sat back in the car. The chauffer shifted gears and turned the steering wheel. The first gate opened slowly onto the street and we rolled back out.

Why this playacting? The Voice must have interfered on my behalf using Its mystic powers, using Its rays to confuse the commanders. The car proceeded slowly around the foot of the wall, as if looking for something.

In the middle of one of the infinite building's wings we found a small iron door. There we stopped. A bronze plaque protruded above the door, but I found it impossible to read the black, oxydized words. I began to feel numb, as if I drank too much wine on an empty stomach.

The sergeant jumped out with the officer again. The same waiting game followed. That bronze plaque probably read: "Crematorium," or "Mental Health Institution."

I strained my eyes until they nearly popped out of their sockets trying to figure out the inscription. The letters blurred, wavered.

"Pray they should not take you inside!" the Voice put my thoughts into words.

What could alter the order given my escorts? What power could change the plan that placed me into this vehicle?

Was this the same crematorium where they took my prisonmates a few days ago to annihilate them? Why did they bring me alive? Was I to act out the last scene of the madness in their "own sphere of jurisdiction?"

Our car idled to be ready for the instant the chauffer received a given signal.

"Just not to this prison!" the Voice tore at my ear.

After a long wait the iron door opened, the civilian and the sergeant returned. The door closed behind them, the sergeant whispered softly to the driver who shifted into high gear and turned back to the city.

* * *

In my old cell, the only change I noticed was a white powder strewn all around the wall: disinfectant? bug killer? or poison? Gratitude flooded over me for returning. I watched the lightplays of the electric bulb, the "light bars" etched into my mind hundreds of times, the bloodstained, graphite-scribble-filled dirty walls, the cot with the pile of covers thrown onto it. Home.

Soon they led me upstairs for a shower, the first one in two months. The warm water caressed my head. The screams of the plumbing distorted the Voice's remarks. Did they want to scald me? I would be helpless even if they decided to pour sulphuric acid over my head. I finished my shower and stood naked on the cold stone. The spitting one kicked my stinking old rags back to me. They could hardly be called clothes any more.

Somehow I had to escape. The Voice and I made the plans. This underground cell could only be downtown. The corridor window came to mind again. Daylight occasionally managed to sneak in through the slits of the planks across it. It had to lead to the outside world. A strong iron door separated us from the upstairs. Whenever I went to interrogation, or to the bathroom, I had to go through that door.

I remembered the guard had not removed the key when he took me to the shower.

I had the solution.

If I could lock the guard on the wrong side of the door and then pry open the window, I could reach the outside world.

I had to try it. I knocked for the guard. The young one came; the one who beat me with the key-ring.

"I have to go to the bathroom," I said. He obliged me, silently waiting outside, watching to see if I repeated yesterday's trick of kicking the toilet bowl. I received a few blows with the billy club for that one.

Returning, I walked in front of him. At the bottom of the stairs, I turned and pulled the iron door shut, I tried to lock it. The guard grabbed the door handle and pulled the door back before I could manage to lock it. I pulled with all my might to shut the door again and turn the key, but the lock caught the air instead of its casing. The guard proved stronger. He opened the door wide and the billy club in his hand swung at me. He swore under his breath, his blows falling on me helter-skelter.

When I fell to the floor, he dragged me into my cell.

My failure hurt me more than the blows or the pouring blood. The evil-faced sergeant made an extra trip to my cell to give me a punch in the face. He knocked me out completely.

"At least these guards believe you are a madman," the Voice comforted me. "Whoever tries to break out of an AVH prison must be mentally unstable."

When the evil-faced one peeked in I yelled: "Rat!" and pointed to the corner of my cell. I followed the trail of my imaginary rat as if I wanted to catch him. "There he is!... And there's another one!"

Secretly I smiled at my primitive game.

The ridiculous trick had greater effect than I expected. A few hours later they led me into the doctor's room again. I repeated my rat-act in front of the Spanish-faced lieutenant colonel, but my eyes were glued to his needle as if hypnotized by it. The Voice kept warning me against needles.

The doctor waited and watched as I bent to the ground in search of the rats.

The Voice prompted me to stand up.

"See, Doctor, I know I pretended to be a fool. The person who knows he is imitating a madman cannot be one himself. It's all a lie."

"What happened to your head?" he asked as he put away the syringe with one hand.

The evil-faced one answered: "A small accident. I put iodine on it and brought him up to you to be treated, comrade lieutenant colonel."

True, he put iodine on my head, but he lied when he said he brought me to the doctor on his own.

CLOSER TO THE LIGHT

End of December, 1952

I slept through the night without an injection.

After breakfast the evil-faced guard came to get me, dressed in his coat and fur hat. He handcuffed me, took me out to the street and pushed me into a windowless paddy wagon. He locked the door from the inside and sat on the bench opposite me.

"What if I hit him over the head?" I wondered, as the thought of escape flashed through my mind again.

Even if I managed to break out of the car, where could I run? Would one of the foreign embassies take me in, if I could find them?

I realized there was no sense in my trying to escape. Maybe they were taking me to the judge. I hoped they had finished my cruel preparation and decided they would not send me to hell "under their own jurisdiction" after all.

The truck stopped after a long hour's rattling. It backed up. Commands sounded. This enormous building was no courthouse.

Two AVH soldiers led me through stern corridors into a cell. To my utter surprise this place looked more like a suite than a cell: it had a window — a real window. The light actually shone through the dense, but thin iron bars. The bed was not a bare plank, but an over-stuffed straw mattress. A white sheet peeked out from under the gray cover. A new gray felt summer coat lay waiting for me. I thanked the Voice in tears for this change in my conditions.[1]

I felt content, but I could not help feeling impatient waiting for action, for the conclusion of my case.

If I received the coveted publicity of a typical showcase trial, I had my plans. I would shout to the whole world about the lawlessness, the illegalities. My own example would be the perfect proof. Not one country in the world permits someone to be kept secretly in jail for six months.

I would list all the other terrors as well: the banishments to the Yugoslavian border region, the poisonings, the disappearances of those internally exiled, and people beaten to death in prisons.

I paced back and forth. My self-confidence inflated as a whole flock of AVH flooded my cell. There were three high-ranking officers

---

[1] The cell I considered so superior turned out to be in the "Small Jail" building (the death row) of the Concentration Jail.

with gold epaulets and some twelve lower-ranking ones. A short civilian wearing a leather cap led them.

"So you are the one?" he asked in a stern, but not unfriendly voice.

Who could this man be? He was no reporter, no true civilian. They did not enter AVH prisons unmolested. He could only have been a high-ranking AVH official. How should I address him? Should I dazzle him with the omniscience of the Voice?

"Yes, Major!" I answered.

He did not reject my guess. One of the AVH officers raised his head in astonishment, but did not dare interrupt.[2]

"See what a nice cell we gave you?" Leather-cap asked. "You have a neat bed and you will receive books. Do you have any wishes?"

"Yes! I would like to get the daily papers, including Western ones."

Leather-cap swallowed. "We'll think about that."

"I have this right, Major. In France, Duclos, the Party Secretary of the French Communist Party, was arrested and held for a few days. He protested when he did not receive his mail one day. I have not read any newspapers and I have received no word about my family for six months. I want to talk to my wife and a lawyer."

"We will think about that also."

They left in a procession.

Beans covered with a tasty onion sauce lured my appetite. Before the Voice could say anything I gulped it down.

In the afternoon a tiny ray of sunshine ventured in through the corner of the window. It warmed body and soul; a tremendous step towards the light.

They left me alone. Late in the afternoon the guard asked me if I felt thirsty. To my affirmative answer he handed me a mess tin with water. After the first swallow I noticed the strange medicine-like taste of the water. It was bitter, nauseating. I knocked for the guard and said: "They put something into my water. I will not drink it!"

He took the mess tin without a word. In a few moments a second lieutenant stood in front of me.

"I am the officer on duty," sounded the unusual introduction. "Why won't you drink your water?"

"There is medicine, or poison in it."

---

[2]The leather-capped civilian proved to be a major indeed, named Bankuti. Between 1950-1953 he was the commander of the biggest jail in Budapest, the Concentration Jail. He ordered the beating to death of a political prisoner who tried to escape. He was also responsible for the so-called "cabbage battle." The latter became infamous because Bankuti ordered the mass beating of those prisoners who refused to eat some inedible cabbage.

"You don't say!"

"May I get water from the tap? Or, maybe you would like to taste this one."

"You are allowed to drink only what the guard gives you."

"Well, I won't drink this, here."

He shrugged and left.

I sensed my problems had just begun. Reading the papers, getting letters seemed light years away. Having allowed me to take a step towards the light, I wondered how much darker my inherent shadows would become?

The door flew wide open and the flock of AVH men who visited me in the morning poured in through it.

"Why don't you drink your water?" Leather-cap yelled at me.

"Because it is poisoned!"

He jumped at me and hit me in the face with his fist. Blood gushed forth from my nose.

"Bring a glass of water," he commanded. "I warn you, here you have to drink and eat anything we give you. I also warn you, you cannot shout here."

They brought the water. He took it and pushed it into my hand.

"Now you will drink it, here, in front of me! Understand?"

I drank it.

"It had no taste!" I told the truth.

"You see," he accepted my praise. "Don't yell now, or I'll drug you with injections."

When the door closed behind them I gave up hope of ever getting any newspapers, legal treatment, or a visit from my wife.

Soon the game with the drinking water started all over. During the group appearances, a white coat would invariably show up behind the behind the door. I had also heard the voice of a woman, talking to the guard. I could not believe my ears: a nurse? here?

Dinner tasted as strangely as the water had before. I received cold creamed potatoes, but I stopped eating after the first bite. The visit with the second lieutenant repeated itself. He threatened me, saying: "The jail commander will feed you!" This had to be Leather-cap.

Nevertheless, I did not touch the food. Leather-cap did not come immediately; he made me wait.

The outside light disappeared into the shadows of the night. Only the strong electric bulb over the door spread its light over me in the accustomed way. The guard brought me a volume of poems by a Stalin Prize winning poet. I hadn't the nerve to read. The nurse whispered something in the corridor. The AVH soldier's monotonous watch through the peephole bothered me. He warned me several times that I would eat or there would be trouble.

"I will not eat it! It is poisoned!" I repeated stubbornly.

A bucket smelling of chlorine stood in the corner. Its strong odor disturbed me, but I preferred it to the stink of excrement. I had just finished adjusting my brand new felt suman-coat when the door flew open. Some eight people poured into the cell, Leather-cap leading the way.

"Why don't you eat?" he hissed in the middle of the cell. Then, without waiting for an answer he pointed at the mess tin. "Pick it up!"

I didn't budge. He picked it up and shoved it in my hand. Then he punched me in the stomach. I staggered and felt buzzing bees circling my head. Leather-cap plunged the spoon into the food. He stuffed it in my mouth and said: "Swallow it! Right now!"

"You may eat it!" the Voice decided. "He will not poison you in front of this many people."

I swallowed the potatoes. Leather-cap gave the mess tin to the officer on duty. "If he yells, he gets an injection!" he declared, turning back from the door.

Through the barred window a deep blue night bent over me. The clear, sparkling clean, cold December night wiped away the remainders of the afternoon sun. The closed window did not shut out the voices of people unloading coal, chunks of it falling off their shovels. I could not understand what the workers said, but I enjoyed hearing the voices of other human beings.

I tried to guess whether the voices belonged to prisoners or free workers, whether outside my window was a street or the yard of the jail. The white-coated girl behind my cell-door represented another puzzle.

My questions bombarded the Voice, but its avoidance of straight answers made me ill at ease. I wanted to see the newspapers because I needed to know if I was still kept secretly, of if my case was covered by the press.

I did not want to give any more signs of life. I was afraid Leather-cap would keep his promises. Nevertheless, the Voice did not let me rest. It commanded, threatened, begged.

I had to act. I jumped onto my bed and yelled at the top of my lungs so the outside coal shovelers could also hear my voice: "Political prisoners! They have kept me, Tottosy, shut off from the world for the past six months. I am Tottosy! Tottosy!... "

A lance sergeant with an enormous head burst into the cell, accompanied by the guard on duty. They pushed me down onto the bed, took off my heavy walking boots and hit my head and body with them.

"Why do you yell, you dog?"

They pulled off the sheet and wrapped it around my neck. Even though they choked me, I did not lose consciousness. I suppressed my moaning. They stopped only when they tired of hitting me. As they left the lance sergeant promised to "stretch me out" if I started over.

I knew I would. Even if the Voice had helped me get above ground and my cell now had a window that let in the light, even if a white sheet covered my straw mattress, I was still kept illegally in secret imprisonment.

The Voice obviously had done much for me. These shadows of AVH who hung around me didn't even guess they couldn't make a step without being noticed, recorded and filmed by the Machine. I came to regard the Machine as one with the Voice. It no longer interested me what its method or its tools were, only the essence mattered, namely my partner: the Voice.

It occurred to me that I should demonstrate to the AVH the power of the Machine, threaten them through some extraordinary exhibition. I would start by guessing their thoughts with the help of the Voice. That should show them!

It pleased me that more people knew about me than merely the AVH officers and guards. Last time I opened my mouth, the coal shoveling stopped. Whoever shoveled coal could only be on our side. No one among the new ruling class shoveled coal.

I stood on my bed. "I, Tottosy have been held under lock and key for the past six months... I demand to be taken to the major!"

I didn't stand for long. Before I had time to notice, the lance sergeant and the guard on duty knelt on top of me. Again, they used my boots to hit me and choked me with my sheet.

"If you say as much as one more word, you dog,... " the lance sergeant panted. He didn't finish his sentence. For some unknown reason he took the sheet off of me. The Voice signaled: they would take me to the major.

"Come!" he said in an ice-cold tone. He grabbed my arm and dragged me to the corridor. For a fleeting moment, I could peek into the cell beside mine that served as the doctor's office. A blond girl in a white coat stood beyond the doorway.

We passed an infinite number of cells, then we walked through linoleum covered corridors. The lance sergeant held my neck as if he carried a fat goose. The Voice kept me from tearing myself out of his grip while we walked down the narrow staircase, through the poorly lit hallways. I wanted to run away, to God only knew where. No way led out from here.

A wide corridor followed, then we entered an elegantly furnished room. Leather-cap sat among cozy bourgeois furniture, behind a carved wooden desk. Another officer was present, but I could not make out his rank.

"What do you want from me?" he asked in an unusually friendly tone.

"See?" the Voice sounded triumphant. "See how polite he is?"

"I wanted to talk to you, Major!" I blurted.

"About what?"

"I wanted to let you know that I..." I got stuck. I had to wait for the Voice's permission to give proof of my special ability to the AVH.

"... I can read people's thoughts, Major."

"You don't say..."

"You don't believe it, Major?"

"No!"

"May I prove it?"

"Try."

"Major, how do I know your rank?"

He suddenly raised his head, but did not answer. He obviously could not hear the malicious remarks with which the Voice accompanied this show of power.

"Do you want me to tell you what is going on with your family?" I continued with my dangerous exhibition.

"Let me hear!"

"Your little girl is expecting you home... "

He nervously waved me away: "Enough! This is nonsense! I warn you for the last time not to shout any more. Dismissed!"

The sergeant grabbed my arm and led me away as if I were blind.

By the time I reached my cell, my feelings of security vanished. I did not know how convincing my mind-reading proofs were. I had to return to my most powerful weapon: giving signs of life from my cell.

The coal shovelers had already heard me and knew my story. I did the best I could.

At the urging of the guard, I took the water offered. It tasted of medicine again, just as bitter as it had been the first time.

I gave it back to him because the Voice urged me to give another sign of life. Although I shook with fear, I had to hurry if I wanted the coal shovelers to hear. I jumped on top of the bed and pulled down the arm of the vent-hole so my voice would carry farther in the silence of the prison night. Although the vent-hole didn't work, my voice sounded louder than ever when I started my usual text: Political prisoners! I..."

They attacked me instantly. The lance sergeant had a yellow coat with him. It looked like a bag. "Straitjacket" — I moaned instinctively. They seized my arms and pulled them into the bag, then tied them to my back. The lance sergeant grabbed my head and pushed it farther and farther back.

"What do they want?" the Voice screamed Its danger signal, "Do they want to choke you? Pray!"

My throat tightened, they kept pushing my head backwards. Rings of fire danced in my eyes ever faster and more blinding. The light turned to white, like the last sudden burst of the lightbulb's filament, and the twirling rings of fire plunged down with me into the deep.

Darkness enveloped everything. the comfortable blackness of unconsciousness, devoid of all sensation, embraced me.

The light went out.

AMONG THE CONDEMNED

Daylight filtered in through the barred window. Fragments of the weak December sunlight brightened my cell. The first thing that caught my eye was the mess-tin filled with black coffee.

"Drink it!" the guard instructed.

I ate the small piece of bread he handed me. I remembered the "stretching out" of last night with a deadly tiredness. I survived it, I had only lost consciousness. My eyes stopped on the volume of poetry at the end of my bed. It lay there neglected like an unknown intruder. The work of a recent notable, it achieved publication not for the talent of its author, but because of the poet's adherence to the Party line. I wanted to ask for a different book. I leaned on my elbow and stared at the guard.

"My goodness!" I grabbed my throat. No sound came out of it. They must have ripped my vocal cords.

I strained as hard as I could, but all my efforts ended in a hoarse, *inarticulate moaning.*

Had the guard known what happened to me? He examined me for a few seconds, then left me alone. Soon he reappeared with the blond girl. Her white nurse's coat inspired trust. A woman who dedicated her life to helping sick people must understand pain. I stepped to her full of hope. I pointed to my throat, like the victim who uncovers his bleeding wound.

"You rotten shit!" the girl said for openers.

In her, I met the reality of my days head on. My hope evaporated like ether. The saving angel of nursing turned into a cruel witch.

"You are lucky to be alive!" she looked me up and down. "It would have been no loss. You should be happy I didn't push that injection up your asshole. From that... " Without finishing her sentence, she shrugged and stalked away, leaving me behind.

My misery occupied me completely. I rubbed my Adam's apple and tried to make sounds, but my best efforts resulted in animal moans. I tried again. I hoped they had only stretched my vocal chords. In vain — I could not even whisper.

They had robbed me of my last weapon: I could no longer give signs of life.

I hoped the coal shovelers who had worked under the prison window carried my message to the world. Yet, I had no way of knowing whether my desperate words would ever reach anyone who'd be interested in freeing me; someone, like a good friend, a client, a humanitarian organization, or a secret member of the resistance. Even if my communication reached them, was there any person who still had courage to attempt to save me? Maybe a doctor could transfer me to the prison hospital. Even if he performed some unnecessary surgery I might be better off than in this hell, sprinkled with unknown dangers. I had to get out of here, no matter how.

The rude-faced sergeant came in dressed in a Russian style fur cap and winter clothes. He led me through corridors and a stony yard in the dry cold which marked the beginning of the Hungarian winter. We passed through an immense iron door, a long corridor, and walked past loitering guards. Finally we reached a giant auditorium containing a several storied gallery-like structure with innumerable doors. Undoubtedly this was a prison; but which one? Whom did all these cell doors hide?

The sergeant pushed me into a small room and yelled: "Take off your clothes!"

On the floor, as if someone had prepared it for me, I found white underwear with a drawstring, frayed suman pants with dirtspots and a worn prisoner's coat. I had to take off my nice, new coat, as well as the rest of the clean pieces of clothing I had received only the day before. Yesterday I must have been more valuable to them. Who understood the mechanism or the logistics of these orders?

I dressed. The sergeant grabbed me by the arm and pulled me around the gallery that housed the jungle of cells. Whenever we passed the middle of the building a red light went on. At this, the guards started to shush and all living beings disappeared from the corridor.

My escort led me into a cell on the main floor.

Outside the dense iron bars, a sheet of tin or wood covered the window. Above the door the inevitable 100 Watt lightbulb glared. The cot was cemented to the floor, but a white sheet and a folded blanket lay on the straw mattress.

"Are they preparing you for the great trial?" the Voice took me to task.

The guard gave me noodles covered with red jam. I waited for instructions from the Voice. Heeding the experiences of the past six months, I knew I had to be suspicious of everything. I guessed we were close to the end of December. Outside there might be snow, the smell of pine trees, maybe even Christmas.

I shook my head to chase away life's temptations. For me the only reality was represented by these noodles covered with red jam.

"I will not touch it. I am sure they must have mixed something into it," I muttered to the Voice.

It couldn't answer because the guard entered and offered me books. According to regulations, a prisoner held by the AVH should not be allowed to have access to books. I tried to rationalize why I had received books, and found no answer. Obviously I was in prison, among the condemned. The guards could not change the order of the prison on account of me alone.

Despite my great thirst for the written word, neither Dickens' short stories, nor the more voluptuous volume, "Stalin: The Questions of Leninism" aroused my interest. I knew I would not be able to concentrate. I could not even pay attention to the Voice. Its questions and answers confused me. Its instructions became uncertain.

The blond nurse stood in the doorway between two guards. She pushed a mess-tin in front of me. Some kind of a liquid splashed around in it.

"Drink it! Don't be afraid!" she pushed it under my nose. "I won't poison you. It's a pain killer, you need it." She pushed the rim of the mess-tin to my lips. I gave in to her strict command. The liquid had a disagreeable medicine-like taste.

She pointed to my mess-tin and said: "Eat your noodles, the jam will take away the taste of the medicine."

I moaned my affirmative answer. When the door closed behind her I tasted the noodles, then ate every bit and licked the bowl.

* * *

Two weeks later the noodles were covered with the same red jam. The Voice comforted me: "It is not blood."

I stretched my neck, like a goose taking big hard swallows. My tortured vocal cords still hurt. I still did not know whether I would ever be able to utter a human sound again. Every time I tried to talk, I ended up moaning. So much anger welled up inside me I almost burst.

The books my guards gave me lay intact on the other empty cot in my cell. The Voice appeared and threatened or urged me only from a foggy distance.

I didn't give up trying and finally, one day, I succeeded in groaning the first word. I repeated it, fretting it might be a hallucination. First I whispered, then I amplified to a jubilant: "Yes."

"Yes!... Yes!" I repeated with redoubled zeal.

I hadn't been silenced forever after all!

I spent the whole day in careful experiments. I increased the volume more and more daringly. I thanked Providence with a heartfelt prayer for again being stronger than all evil.

In three days, I spoke entire sentences out loud again. On the fourth day the blond witch must have sensed my improvement.

"Can you speak now?" she asked when she administered my medication.

"A little."

"Don't you dare shout again."

The next two days I barely talked with the Voice. Whether it was the influence of the medicine, or my general weakness, I spent two nights in dazed sleep. Every noon I drank the bad-tasting medicine without protest.

On the third evening, during the distribution of dinner, I felt the sad reality of this huge prison for the first time. The banging of doors, the wandering noises of the giant kettles from which they dished out our meals and the smell of the food all reminded me of my incarceration.

"Here I am again!" the Voice returned with renewed vitality. "What do you think, did the medicine work?" It mocked me by emphasizing the word "medicine."

"I don't know," I reacted, giving way to a burst of insecurity.

"Do you have strength to fight for your life?"

I shuddered. Must we start this pretend madness again?

"There are thousands of condemned here, they will all one day return to the world."

"So?"

"You must give them a sign of life."

"And my trial?"

"Are you thinking about the trial of your case?" It asked disapprovingly. "You don't imagine they are going to take you straight to the prosecutor?"

"They won't?"

"No, my friend!... They can 'settle you within their own jurisdiction.' They can poison, beat or choke you to death... Nobody knows you are here."[1]

The Voice only confirmed my fears. But why did they move me from one prison to another, from one cell to another?

"Why did they bring you here?" the Voice posed the most important question.

The public told horror stories about the AVH prisons in both Szombathely and Veszprem. People avoided even the vicinity of these jails;

---

[1] In Budapest, the court tried the case of the Balazs's who attempted to leave the country illegally with me. The Balazs's received small punishments. The AVH summoned my wife several times and questioned her about me. Her lawyer reported I had escaped to Paris and lived there with a dancing girl. My family, naturally, received no sign of life from me. After the half-official confirmation of my escape, my family became increasingly convinced that I was dead.

they were dreaded as much as the AVH Headquarters, at 60 Andrassy Avenue in Budapest. God only knew for certain how many cellar prisons existed.

"Not even you, a lawyer, knew about their existence. I bet the bar association doesn't know about them either," the Voice mocked.

"Get undressed and go to bed!" the guard commanded through the food window.

I threw down my suman coat and coarse felt pants, then slid under my blanket. The comfortable coolness of the sheet chased away my fright for the moment.

"Listen!" I heard the abhorred instruction, "you will pretend you are crazy!"

I didn't protest.

"Sit up in your bed and shout as loud as you are able. Say your name!" I complied.

"Tell them, you, as a lawyer, know the law and the law states that any arrested person has to be brought in front of a prosecutor within three days of his arrest. Tell them you have been arrested for months and that you had not seen anyone, neither lawyer, nor prosecutor, nor relatives!"

I shouted as the Voice ordered me, my words breaking through the iron door.

"Tell them their tortures are against international law!" The Voice led me to increasingly daring attacks. "The AVH policemen will be hanged like the war criminals at the trial at Nuremberg."

The words terrified me. I shouted to the terror in power that international vengence waited for them. I screamed more than heresy, I called out in provocation!

They took me in my shirt and underwear, across the center of the prison, to a brightly lit doctor's office.

The Spanish-faced lieutenant colonel of the medical corps looked me over. His elegant uniform, shiny boots, the glistening of his gold epaulets, his sternly shut ascetic lips constituted a clear contrast with the gray brutality of the guards who dragged me into his office. The doctor looked like an indifferent medical researcher personified, watching me as if he observed a guinea pig.

"Why are you yelling?" he calmly asked.

"Do you hear what he just said?" the Voice pounced on me. "He does not say you pretend to be mad, because he has to stick to his role of the practicing physician."

He played around distractedly with a syringe.

"Lieutenant colonel..." I started. "I already asked you..."

"What?"

"I asked you not to give me injections. I do not want to lose my identity, I want to remain a human being! Once you granted my wish!"

"Then, why do you shout?"

"I have to give a sign of life."

"Keep quiet!"

He did not inject me.

When the yellow-haired nurse brought me medicine again, she doubled my dose. I took it anyway. Two days passed without new incidents. The Voice even agreed to let me finish half my lunch.

However, at night It insisted I start shouting again. After my name, I yelled that AVH men will be hanged by their feet.

Where did I get that nonsense? Why and who would hang them by their feet? Maybe I was repeating things I heard from the loudspeaker at the Veszprem prison. Hanging people by their feet sounded like a crazy nightmare.[2]

What did the AVH guards feel when I yelled this? In this giant prison all guards were AVH policemen and not ordinary prison guards. The AVH guarded the condemned even after they were sentenced by the court. The only way out of their grasp led to the cemetery.

The guards fell onto me again, breaking into my daydreams. They dragged me to the doctor's office where the civilian chief doctor expected me. I hadn't seen him for quite some time, but I remembered his frog eyes.

"Why are you yelling again?" he screeched at me. "What do you want to achieve with this shouting?"

"To give a sign of life! Why don't you try my case?"

"That does not depend on us."

"But my life depends on you. Don't let them give me any injections."

He didn't answer.

I began to realize that all this medical charade was a well-planned alibi. If, one night, in the course of an interference, a guard killed me, they already averted all responsibility by establishing my medical condition. My trial might never come. They brought me here, as if I had had a trial already, ready to "settle my case under their own jurisdiction" through the medical form of beating me to death.

"Some day you will find out the whole truth!" my ethereal friend repeated Its usual refrain.

---

[2]Unfortunately, during the 1956 Uprising, the anger and the hatred against the AVH led the people — in isolated cases — to lynch and hang some of the AVH officers by their feet.

THE NAMELESS

January, 1953

After "reveille" the guard brought a tall broad-shouldered prisoner into my cell. He wore prison garb and carried his only possession, his mess-tin, in his hand.

"I brought you a partner! See that you get along!"

I scrutinized the newcomer. He did not introduce himself, did not even offer his hand to shake. In jail, people were herded in and out like animals, there seemed to be no need for manners.

"Don't talk to him!" the Voice commanded. "Wait a while... "Who do you think that man could be? Watch him!"

After months of solitary confinement, I regarded this partner warily. He showed very little interest in my identity.

"They must have told him all about you," the Voice continued.

"What is your name?" I asked the newcomer.

"What does it matter? I am a prisoner."

His cold rejection did not invite further conversation. I never again asked his name or his case. He remained the "Nameless" for me. I examined his features with the passion of a scientist. His blue eyes sparkled in an intelligent, clean-shaven face. His strict facial expression had the pretense of boredom written all over it.

Despite my distrust and without any connection, the Voice urged me to talk about the Machine. It wanted me to reveal my special talent of reading people's thoughts to my new partner. I wanted to show him the source of all my talents: the Machine.

He listened attentively.

"What does your miracle machine tell you about me?" he asked arrogantly.

"You are a stool-pigeon!" I said mechanically, on cue, repeating what the Voice had just told me.

He threw back his head. I waited for his long arms to grab me and make me pay for the rudest offense in prison life. He didn't react. He stood up when we heard the clinking of keys as if he knew they came for him. the guard poked in his head: "Come, time for your walk!" he said to Nameless.

A walk — to breathe fresh air... When the AVH brought me to Budapest by car, I took only a few steps outside. I walked from the building, across the yard with the wild chestnuts, straight to the car. I dreamed that walk, smelled that walk. The guard took Nameless for a walk, I stayed in our festering cell.

Shortly after his walk, we received our lunch. His double portions proved he had connections in the right places!

The blond nurse brought my usual daily medicine.

"Be careful with him!" she said to Nameless while she handed me the mess-tin.

Nameless received double portions at night again. He must have needed it. He looked three times my size. His presence and the weight of the mystery that surrounded him almost made me forget the Voice.

Our prison garbs rested neatly folded at our feet and I turned against the wall, awaiting the salvation of sleep, when desperate shouting woke me from my slumber.

"I beg of you... I can't stand it any longer! No more! Don't do it any more."

The moaning sounded again. Then from afar, in a completely different tone, another one, then a third. Each of them begged: "No more... !"

But what "no more?" Only weak murmurs answered the tortured victims' choking, painful moans.

I shook under the cover as I tried to find an answer — in vain. My familiar Voice chose not to come to my rescue.

* * *

The Voice remained silent for a week, — forever?

Nameless slowly opened up, but he never told me his name. The conversations filled the emptiness of my days. I found my partner perfect for pretentious discussions. A convinced Marxist, he indiscriminately hated everything he considered "the old world." He almost bragged about being present at the execution of the war criminals. I did not ask him in what capacity.

Unexpectedly, he wanted to talk about Christ. With no intention to mock, rather to debate, he took a cold, scientific approach. His forehead wrinkled when I spoke about the fiascos of Christianity, but his face betrayed no sense of glory. He did not become cynical when I confessed to Christian people's human weaknesses.

Two world views collided in our discussions. We fenced, in prison-garb, without swords, titles, or positions. The steel of our arguments sparked, but the eyes of Nameless caught fire only when he felt he had no answers to my questions.

He turned his probing to my private life. He inquired about my personal fate, my partners, and my case. I sensed the fine maze of interrogation in his manner. He wanted to take my secrets and use them for himself.

Occasionally, they took him away for hours. I just knew: on these occasions he was writing about me, confessing who knew what.

About a week later they took me to Sir again. He seemed to follow wherever they took me.

"You have a companion!" Goat-chin started.

"Yes!"

"A few days ago you yelled again."

"Only to give a sign of life."

"What for?"

I didn't want to answer; I missed the Voice who would have had a fitting reply for me. I had to be on my guard. I could not guess what Sir knew.

"We are investigating your case," he said. "Are you getting books?"

"Yes."

"I'll see you again, soon."

This short conversation made no sense.

Nameless didn't ask me where I went or what happened. We lived in separate worlds that stood not side by side, but opposite one another.

I forgave him. I found it amusing how faithfully he protected the Communist social order. I had imagined that anyone convicted by them would hate and oppose them. This man, however, agreed with every one of their limitations of individual human rights, with their cruelly enforced regulations. Even as their victim, he approved of everything about the system.

"If you think the system is so perfect, why did you commit a crime against it?" I asked him point-blank.

"I didn't!"

"You didn't? Then why are you here?"

He angrily waved away my question and stared at the blind window. Our conversation died for the time. He pulled the sheet over his face, so the light should not bother him. I turned to the wall to avoid the stale, chlorine smell of the bed-linen.

In the evening, the mysterious moanings sounded again. Two people shouted in pain and begged with the usual choking groans.

"Do you hear it?" I asked Nameless.

"I hear it!" he answered from under the sheet. "So what?"

"How can you say 'so what'? They are torturing those people."

"It's not torture, they punish them," he said, lifting his sheet to show me his disgust.

"Punish them?"

"Yes, for disobeying."

"How can it possibly be punishment? This is torture!"

"To put somebody in irons is a disciplinary punishment."

"What does that involve exactly?" I asked cautiously. He turned back his sheet and propped himself up on his elbow.

"They tie their hands together and chain them to their outstretched legs," he explained indifferently.

The lawyer in me revolted. I was shocked to see medieval methods revived in our legal system.

"Do you really think it's legal?"

"Why not, if they break the prison rules?"

"It's medieval to put people in irons."

"Middle Ages, or fascist opposition — it doesn't make any difference. Whoever breaks the rules has to be punished."

My anger burst out: "That's inhumanly painful!"

"Some take it for a long time, others faint pretty fast."

I closed my eyes; I remembered the horror of my days in the cellar. I guess it worked with me. I no longer yelled my name at night. Torture for the AVH not only served to extricate confessions from people, but also to silence their lawful demands.

"See," the Voice returned clearly and in full force. "You are material for a special procedure. What a good question for the Machine to answer. How are they building their People's Paradise?"

I listened in contented, uncomfortable silence.

The Voice's presence swept away my sense of helplessness, but its nameless cynicism never failed to make me angry. While the miserables moaned inside these walls, jovial lecturers and well-paid professors praised the economy, the economic achievements of the three and five year plans, the socialist self-consciousness of those marching in front of Rakosi on designated national holidays. The Voice swept past my burning sense of injustice.

I understood the plans of the Machine. Someone, maybe several people, had to walk this inner, secret calvary to preserve its methods in the form of tapes, pictures, films. The purpose of this procedure was to reveal to the world the anachronistic, medieval methods used to build a society that surpassed even the Middle Ages in its cruelty and backwardness. The reason the Voice conjured up the vision of Stalin's "truth villages" became quite clear to me. It simply mocked me! The moments in which I saw everyone and everything as good perverted reality. In those confused moments, my naive human soul could believe that Stalin was capable of good deeds. In reality he had exiled, locked away from the world and destroyed many millions of human beings. Many people knew it and talked about it, yet the world did not want to believe it. It was much simpler to deny it, or to ignore the facts.

Individuals, titles, methods may have changed, even terror might have taken on different forms, but the essence remained. That is why my witness was needed.

I had to follow my mission to the end. I was a mere instrument and the instrument could not revolt against its imposed destiny. The fate of others depended on me. I had to shout for them also.

"Shout! Hurry!" the Voice whistled in my ear.

"Political prisoners!" I yelled at the top of my lungs. "The AVH will have to answer for its tortures in front of an international tribunal. To put people in irons is against the law and is inhuman. I... "

Nameless leaped out of bed, his eyes flaming. He sealed my mouth with his enormous palm. I managed to pull away my head.

"The inquisitors will be hanged! I... "

My time ran out. He beat my head with his walking boots. He hit me in the face and did not stop when blood spurted from my nose.

"Take that, and that, you bastard... you deserve it all. How do you dare to say such a thing... "

For the first time someone put his entire hatred into the beating. With the guards, I had always felt order as the deciding factor. Their blows and tortures addressed a dangerous animal they needed to stop.

Nameless, on the other hand, beat me with the anger of fanaticism, with the rage of an offended ideologist, with the wild hatred directed towards a "counter-revolutionary." I was an enemy on whom he could revenge himself.

His identity no longer presented a puzzle: he showed his true colors.[1]

---

[1] According to later stories told by my prison-mates and based on the description I gave them, my cell-mate was an AVH colonel, convicted in connection with the Rajk case, then used as a stool-pigeon to spy on a few select prisoners.

STRAITJACKET AND FORCEFEEDING

January and February, 1953

My head throbbed. Amidst the clinking of watercans, Nameless swiftly took in the daily portion of water. Antipathy, wrapped in silence, stretched between my partner and myself. I found it unthinkable to continue our discussions.

"You want to talk with this one?" the Voice intoned Its first question of the day. "He introduced himself last night! I warned you about him. He's a stool-pigeon."

It was right. Last night Nameless pounced on me like a vulture after my first cry. They must have commanded him to immediately choke back my first words of revolt. Why didn't they put me into irons as they had done with the others? What was the explanation for the nurse's tireless appearance with my daily medication? Did they take me for a madman? Were they "settling my case under their jurisdiction" by murdering me with a slow-killing poison?

Today, I pretended to swallow the bitter slop, but kept it in my mouth until the door shut behind the girl. Then I spit it into the bucket.

"Did you spit it into the toilet?" Nameless asked, watching me with ogre eyes.

"None of your business!"

He knocked for the guard. He whispered through the half opened door: "He spit it out again."

"I'll report it immediately," the guard answered offhandedly.

We had dry peas for dinner. My cruel partner again received a double portion. Mine came separately, late, just as my soup had come separately in Veszprem, at the AVH Prison.

A few days later everything started.

"Try it... " the Voice warned me.

The dried peas tasted like medicine. Obviously, they had mixed their poison into my food and thought hunger would outweigh caution. I ate only the small piece of bread and put my mess-tin, filled with the dried peas, beside the water-bucket.

"How much longer?" I asked the Voice.

"Do you think it depends on me?"

"How can I hold out to the end? Will there be an end?"

"You must hold out. You see, your shouts for help worked. You managed to get yourself out of the death-cell."

"True."

My disgusting partner was taken for a walk with the rest of the prisoners. Cell doors banged open, the innumerable feet of the prisoners thundered. They must have been forbidden to talk as words never blended with the trampling of their feet.

Without the Voice's prompting, I thought of giving signs of life.

"Do you think it would work?" It asked.

"I don't know."

"Stupid! All the prisoners are outside. You would be yelling to the empty walls."

"Do I have to yell again today?" I asked, hoping for a holiday from torture.

"You'll see!"

I tasted my dinner, feeling the taste of the chemical again. After taps I hurried to get undressed.

"Shout, immediately!... Start with your name!" the Voice roused me as soon as I jumped between covers.

"Political prisoners! I, Tottosy... have been held for more than seven months. That is against the law... "

Nameless sat on my bed, his long fingers clung tightly around my throat: "I'll choke you, you miserable creature!"

"He wouldn't dare! Don't be afraid!" the Voice encouraged me. "If his grasp lightens, shout that your cellmate is choking you... "

I pulled my head back and forth and yelled a few fragmented sentences.

Four guards ran in. A gold-epauleted, gypsy-faced slim second lieutenant led them.

"Rotten bastard!" he dealt me a blow on my head. "How dare you shout again?"

"Second lieutenant," I answered, getting out of the grip of Nameless. "I demand to be taken to the prosecutor. After seven months I have the right to be tried!"

I shouted the sentence as loud as I could so others would also be able to hear it through the open door.

"I'll show you your rights! Tie him up!"

My heart raced. Now they'll put me in irons. They tied only my hands; my matchstick legs dangled freely down the side of the bed.

"What good does this half-hearted work do?" the Voice mocked. "Are you a special prisoner? They do not dare put you in irons?"

However, the further instructions of the second lieutenant shook my belief in being some special prisoner.

"Fascist garbage," he continued. "If I hear your voice just once more, I'll show you how cruel I can get."

I had absolutely no doubts about that.

When the four guards left the cell, Nameless did not lie back down, but put on his prison-coat. To comply with the order to watch over me, he sat staring.

My teeth chattered as I sat there, tied up in my white underwear for hours. Around morning a guard came in alone, untied me and pointed to my bed: "You may lie down now."

Their day was done.

* * *

The next day, then again on the third, I did not have to shout, but the Voice would not let me eat my vegetables, bread, or noodles. Everything went into the toilet.

In the afternoon two prisoners screamed again. Then the silence turned leaden.

Nameless read on his bed. Occasionally he glanced at me. He was prepared to pounce on me any minute I would give him the excuse by crying out. I wondered what his mystery was, what hold the AVH had on him. Although I had learned quite a bit about him during our discussions, I never found out why or how he ended up in prison. Maybe one of the Party's unknown puppeteers grew tired of Nameless' servile intelligence and dealt him the role of the slave. Or, it could have been merely "in the interest of the Party" to make him step down from the stage of life and accept the role of the denounced, self-accusing pretend-criminal.

Was it a coincidence or was it planned that they brought me the account of the Rajk trial to read?[1] I thought increasingly about how the low echelon Party members must have reacted to the imprisonment of Rajk, to his ousting of the Communist Party, to his repentant confessions and hanging. All those, who only days before searched for his good graces, pumping his hand, were they now satisfied with the mere compensation of not being behind bars themselves? Could they make themselves believe that Rajk was a Western agent, not merely a heretic Communist, searching for a Yugoslavian type nationalistic Communist solution for Hungary? Did they actually believe in his being guilty in political terms?

"Did Rajk play a theatrical role?" asked the Voice.

---

[1] Laszlo Rajk was the Minister of the Interior, later Minister of Foreign Affairs of the Communist government. After a repentant confession, the Janko Council condemned him to death on September 24, 1949. His sentence was carried out immediately along with the execution of others sentenced with him. The system rehabilitated Rajk in 1956, before the Revolution. Janko, Chairman of the Council that sentenced him, committed suicide at that time.

"Naturally."

"And Mindszenty?"

"They treated him chemically to prepare him for his trial."

"And Cardinal Grosz, the third great conspirator?"[2]

"He too played a role!"

I answered the Voice's questions with determination. The lessons in inquisition, drawn from the comedies of the court trials of the Hungarian Community,[3] Cardinal Mindszenty,[4] and Rajk, were used with great results in the trial of Cardinal Grosz as well.

Would the trial of our conspiracy be the fifth one in the history of great showcase trials?

The year 1952 had not yet staged its own showcase trial to bring the necessary press sensation and deterrent the Rakosi style permanent revolution so badly needed every year in order to keep functioning. The memories of Cardinal Grosz' conspiracy trial reminded me of the way the blaring Communist press reported these trials.

Endre Farkas, the alleged Attorney General arrested and tried with the Cardinal, had been a friend and colleague. I met him first in the humble conference room of the Ujpest District Court, on a sunny morning, in 1946. He represented my opponent. We introduced ourselves. He hung his black melon-like hat on the back hanger of the conference room. He gave the impression of a retired London banker in his dark, worn suit. He spoke softly as if constantly apologizing, in a disciplined, humble manner.

Under no condition was he a leader, let alone a conspirator trying to topple Rakosi.

"You never believed his guilt?" the Voice followed my thoughts.

"Never! Farkas was swept into the trial through association with Grosz. He had never played any role in politics."

No one took the sad theatrical comedy of the Grosz trial seriously.

---

[2]Archbishop Jozsef Grosz was the successor of the imprisoned Cardinal Mindszenty. The trials of his conspiracy case started in January of 1951. He himself was arrested May 15, 1951. In June he was sentenced to 12 years imprisonment.

[3]The showcase trial of the Hungarian Community (also known as the Hungarian Fraternal Community) was popularly known as the conspiracy trial of colonel-general Lajos dalnoki Veress, a brave and excellent Hungarian soldier who had also been sentenced to death by the Nazi puppet government of Szalasi. The arrests started on December 31, 1946 and the prime accused, Dr. Gyorgy Donath, was executed September 17, 1947.

[4]The first arrest in the showcase trial of Primate Cardinal Joseph Mindszenty, that of Andras Zakar, took place in November 1948. The Cardinal himself was arrested December 26, 1948. His trial was conducted by Vilmos Olty and took place in the Marko Street Court on February 2, 1949. Cardinal Mindszenty and Dr. Bela Ispanky were sentenced to life imprisonment. Bishop Meszlenyi was allegedly killed in the course of the interrogations.

Farkas has recited his repentant memorized confessions with a yellow-white mask-like face. I saw my own face in the same circumstances.[5]

The chills ran up and down my spine. I shook my head.

"Say it won't be so," I cried for help from the Voice.

"Then you have to yell out the truth!" the Voice demanded sternly. As usual, It gave Its orders in the evening.

I sat up. I tore the cover off my white underwear taking no heed of Nameless, sitting on the opposite bed, ready to leap at me.

"Shout your name!" came the usual command.

"Political prisoners, I, Tottosy, have been held seven months..."

My partner, ordered to be my warden, immediately leaped at me and clung to my throat with one hand, while with the other he held his boot tight, ready to shower blows on my head.

I shouted louder.

"The AVH will be accountable for the murders..."

I cannot recall how I slid out from his grip and ran towards the door, so the others outside could hear my voice better.

"Members of the AVH will be hanged, an international tribunal will judge their inhumanities. They will be sentenced like the Nazi war criminals were in the trial at Nuremberg."

I finished my sentence, but Nameless caught up with me and used his boot with purpose.

I struggled to get out from the grip of his tentacle-like arms when the second-lieutenant arrived with his special squad. He carried the straitjacket.

---

[5]Endre Farkas, a Budapest lawyer, was sentenced to life imprisonment in connection with the "Archbishop Grosz conspiracy trial."

In the summer of 1956 we were cell-mates. He told me his story. He was the archbishop's classmate. They became good friends. He frequently visited the archbishop's residence. On such occasions they talked about the fate of the country and the role of the Catholic Church. This was his crime.

After his arrest the AVH informed him about his simple case. He must confess to conspiring to form a counter-government, in which he was to have played the role of Attorney General.

They didn't torture him, they did not touch him. They coldly told him, if he deviated from the prepared text of the confession, he would hang.

He knew — by 1951 everyone knew — he had no choice. If he decided to alter his confession at his showcase trial — in the midst of sensation-hungry reporters — and let the world know he had been forced to falsify the truth, they would immediately take him out and administer the "mental health injection."

When we first met he had been a prisoner for five years — I for four. In those days Archbishop Grosz, a well-known church authority, had already been released for quite some time. Endre Farkas, an ordinary lawyer, could easily be forgotten. His sentence was never revised, only the Revolution of 1956 gave him back his freedom.

After the Revolution was crushed, they took him back to jail. He died there, forgotten.

Four of them had to hold me down. They threw me on my bed and forced me into the yellow linen bag. They pulled my arms through its sleeves, then bound them together on my back. They tied a white kerchief over my mouth. They stiffened me into immobility and silence.

Why did they go through this comedy, fit for a madman, when I was not mad? If I broke the rules they should put me into irons, not into a straitjacket.

"What logic motivates them?" the Voice continued my meditation.

"They must have some secret purpose."

"So?"

"Do they want to prove I am mad?"

"That is not enough," said the Voice. "Why do they poison your food?"

"That's true." Terror struck me.

Four days had passed since I had eaten. I dared to ladle a small drink of water from the bucket only because Nameless drank from that too. That proved to me the bucket was not poisoned.

"They want to make me vanish," the Voice helped me to pronounce my constant fear.

The gypsy second-lieutentant bent towards me. His tiny button eyes sparked with anger: "What did yhou shout, you rotten fascist? I'll take away your mood for yelling!"

He twisted my ear. He jerked it so hard, blood poured down my face. The white kerchief over my mouth even prevented me from crying out my pain.

Then — just for fun — he held my nose so I could not breathe for a few moments. The game brought a smile on his face.

The guards stood around me showing neither sympathy nor antipathy, waiting only for the next command. In all probability, if ordered, they would have choked me. They served as mere cogs in a machine, slaves to their duty, uncaring about men, life, or pain.

Did someone want to convince these automatons I was a madman? They were madmen, the miserable madmen of power.

They let me shiver there for hours tied-up in the straitjacket and my long white underwear, gagged.

Around dawn the officer on duty removed the white rag from my mouth and, with the help of Nameless, he peeled off the straitjacket.

I watched them warily. The guard arranged my covers on me with unusual caring. "You have such nice brown dog-eyes. I won't hurt you," he said.

* * *

They pulled the strait jacket on me again. They pushed a gas mask over my head. This new invention pleased them immensely.

"Who gives them the instructions?" the Voice wondered.

"The doctors."

"The elegant Spaniard, or the fish-eyed one?"

The fish-eyed doctor often accused me of pretending, but if he truly believed that, why did he order regular medical treatment?

The gypsy second lieutenant could not penetrate the world of my thoughts, he just giggled, enjoying his small power. The gas-mask stunk from preservative oil applied in the warehouse. I could breathe only through the small bottom hole intended for the filter; there was no way to shout.

"He looks like a wild hog," the second lieutenant joked.

Two of the guards laughed, the other two exercised restraint.

"Mr. Wild Hog," the second lieutenant mocked, "oink a bit for us, if you can."

He closed off my tiny breathing hole with his hand. He had no intention of choking me, but he found the game amusing. I was bound so tightly in that yellow bag, I could not pull my head away when his dark brown palm stopped my air-flow.

As he left, he counted the mess-tins I had not touched for the past five days. He asked Nameless softly.

"Doesn't this animal eat?"

"No, sir."

They vanished.

The Voice chided me. "He counted your mess-tins. Now they know you are not eating."

I sat on my bed, shivering in the straitjacket, flaunting the head of a wild hog, until reveille when the guard saved me from my misery.

"Did you notice last night?" the Voice reminded me. "He counted your mess-tins. Now they know you are not eating."

Morning coffee arrived.

"Pour it into the toilet!" the Voice ordered.

I looked longingly after my breakfast, but I obeyed. The content of my mess-tin splashed noisily in the bowl. Nameless knocked for the guard and told of my deviation from the rules.

In the afternoon three people came to get me. I followed them to the doctor's office, entirely in control of myself, without being handcuffed. Spanish-face and the blond nurse stood side by side.

"I heard you are not eating," he said.

"True, lieutenant colonel."

"Why not?"

"Because I don't want them to poison me."

"Nonsense."

"Don't you regard my treatment unusual? Why don't they try my case if I am healthy? If I am not, why don't they take me to the hospital? Why am I hidden among the convicted?"

"Who told you... " he started the sentence. He probably wanted to ask how I knew they kept me in a jail for convicts.

"See, he cannot answer," the Voice was jubilant. "Notice how you embarrassed him in front of the guards."

The lieutenant colonel withdrew behind his desk and pretended to look for a syringe.

"You can take him!" he said. "If he does not eat today, we will force him."

Back at my cell the Voice started in on me again.

"Did you see his benevolence? He tries to prove he is only a medical doctor who cares about your life. But that does not mean your situation is not serious."

"Inasmuch as... "

"Even if thousands know you are here, when will they get back outside? They cannot contact anyone, there are no visitors with whom they could send a message."

"Only you can help."

"Yes. I record everything on film, on tape."

"I know."

"Don't even hope that any message will get out of here."

I did not touch my lunch or my dinner.

In the numbing silence after taps, guards circled the jail and passed the cells like ghosts in their felt slippers to catch everything suspicious, even a few bitter sighs. Talk was forbidden, but someone might whisper something: cause for a red alert.

That night the cover of my peephole was repeatedly opened and closed.

"They are afraid you will shout again," said the Voice, picking the words from my mind.

"I don't have to, today?"

I was afraid of the answer; yesterday's wild hog scene wore me out completely.

My struggle took its toll; I could see no light at the end of the tunnel. I pondered how much better it would be to simply be killed one night. I wouldn't have to refuse food any more, this whole hell would be over.

The film, the tapes would survive at any rate; they would suffice to prove the diabolical methods of my tormentors. I had done my job! I had had enough!

"Are you out of your mind?" the Voice retorted. "Do you think this is what they expect from you?... Today you do not have to give a sign of life."

The peephole cover swung open again. Nameless must have noticed it too because he propped himself up on his elbow. He followed my every move like a hungry preybird watches its victim. His gray eyes flashed in warning as if they said: don't even try it!

I spent the night tossing in my bed.

After the morning walk of the convicts, five people crowded into my cell. The nurse made the fifth. A long rubber hose dangled from her hands, she had also brought equipment used for enemas. They held me down on my bed, as they would a patient before surgery.

"Don't you see what they want?" the Voice asked.

"What should I do?"

"Squeeze your mouth shut. Don't let them... don't let them push that rubber hose down your throat."

The nurse bent over me. "Open your mouth, you animal!" she gruffed.

"Don't let her!" the Voice commanded. "You need all your strength. Should they succeed in pouring something into your stomach, their doctor could prove you died from natural causes. Even if you have to die, prove their crimes by dying with an empty stomach."

I did not understand Its reasoning, but I was convinced the Voice knew what I should do. I exercised all my strength to keep my mouth tightly shut.

First they tried to pry my lips open, then they held my nose, I gasped for air, but only through clenched teeth, so they could not push the rubber hose down my throat.

"Good job, be strong!" the Voice encouraged me.

They tried a different tool; they attempted to push a tongue depressor, soaked in something, between my teeth. Its strong taste bit into my gums. Still, I persevered. The nurse took her turn trying to push the tongue depressor between my teeth. She was not the least disturbed by the sight of my bleeding gums. An order is an order! The rubber hose had to go down.

"Clench your teeth!" the Voice ordered. "It doesn't matter if they break a few. Your life is at stake!"

My teeth broke. Two of my torturers forced the tongue depressor through. My resistance faded, I couldn't go on. The rubber hose forged into my throat between my clenched teeth. Some type of cold liquid poured down my throat from the enameled dish the nurse held high.

"It doesn't matter!" the Voice consoled me. "It's understandable you couldn't tolerate it any longer."

I could not breathe.

My body shuddered, I was sweating and panting. When they finally pulled the rubber hose from my throat, I threw up the cold slop onto the floor.

One of the guards took a crumpled up rag and wiped my mouth. He shrugged, as if he expressed his personal opinion: this one is a goner but we carried out the order.

Nameless watched their actions without taking part in them. My half-broken teeth throbbed all night. In the morning the Voice allowed me to eat my bread and gulp down my coffee.

I survived the forcefeeding.

For two days the Voice let me rest.

On the third day, I had to give a sign of life. A round-faced major stormed in leading a detachment of AVH men. One of his ears was missing, as if someone tore it off in a boxing or wrestling match. The gypsy second lieutenant arrived, unwilling to miss the spectacle. The taciturn second lieutenant, who so far had not touched me, rounded out the honor guard.

Four guards stood on the threshold awaiting their orders.

"Pull the straitjacket on him!" the major ordered.

This was the first time they actually called it "straitjacket". They pulled it as hard as they could and tied my hands to my back.

"That too!" the major pointed to the gas mask. "It proved to be a mighty efficient tool." He stopped in front of me, turned his stump of an ear towards the other side and took up a fighter's pose, as if he wanted to knock me over.

"If you shout your name ever again, you rotten... then you will get this from now on!" He took a deep breath. "I am the jail commander, your life depends on me."[6]

The gypsy second lieutenant, trying to show off his humor to the commander, blocked the air-hole on my gas mask again. The silent second lieutenant stood, as if the scene left him completely indifferent.

"If you prefer spending the night like that you are welcome to it," the major said in parting.

In two or three hours the officer on duty came in. The guards changed so often, it was almost impossible for me to identify them. "Can you lie down if I help you get settled? I cannot take off your gas mask yet," he said regretfully.

I nodded. I sensed he had no order for letting me lie down either.

The Voice became curious: "Do you think he knows what is happening to you?"

"I think he feels sorry for me. Maybe he is one of those who was drafted and assigned this duty. Now he merely acts on orders."

---

[6] Janos Bankuti, the leather-capped AVH major, was in the meantime relieved from his duty and became an inmate himself. In the whirl of events I never found out the name of the new commander with the missing ear, a major according to his stripes.

Even when lying down I could not sleep in the straitjacket. My entire costume was not removed 'til morning. "Why do you think they brought you here?" the Voice pounced on me.

"I have no idea." Neither my knowledge as a lawyer, nor my human instincts could find an answer.

"It's incomprehensible," I continued. Mindszenty, Rajk, or Grosz, none of them was locked up before their trial. True; the preparation for their trial was not so long either.

"See, their methods are getting more sophisticated. Now do you see why your testimony is so badly needed?"

* * *

I continued giving signs of life and every time my own threats frightened me. In the course of the following week, they tied me up in the straitjacket five times. The Voice gave me a new command to stop eating. My mess-tins lined up again beside the entrance. Another forcefeeding followed.[7]

The method, the procedure and the result each were the same as the first time, except this time I gave in sooner.

Occasionally, they undressed me and wrapped me in wet sheets; an obvious medical treatment, a proof to their own guards that I was ill, therefore not fit for trial. A good alibi for not taking me to see the prosecutor.

The Voice's explanations no longer satisfied me. I found the situation intolerable. I froze in the unheated cell during the cold months of January and February. I felt tired, weak, and worn.

Something had to happen. I just knew: a ray of hope must be on its way to warm my meager existence.

The Machine mentioned a "death-ray" months ago. Would the Machine's death-ray prove to be my saving angel?

The Voice itself communicated with me through an unknown ray. It seemed quite possible to intensify this ray to the extent that it would paralyze the human body, disable the attacker.

---

[7]This forcefeeding lacking medical supervision caused the death of many.

There were no "hunger strikes" in AVH jails. A hunger-strike loses its meaning if news about it cannot reach the public. No news ever oozed out of AVH prisons.

The forcefeeding described in this chapter was administered according to the methods of the Stalin era.

We have records of another forcefeeding, much later — in 1957, after the death of Beria, in a much laxer period, and after the banishment of the AVH — namely that of Losonczi, a former Communist minister, during the trial of Imre Nagy, Prime Minister during Hungary's four days of freedom. Losonczi died because of that forcefeeding.

"Do you want to threaten them?" the Voice asked.

"Would it work?"

"Fear can stop evil."

Self-confidence seeped through my wasted body.

Lunch didn't taste of medicine, so I ate it. I received no medication in the morning either. Nameless immersed himself in his reading and became watchful only when I approached the door.

I waited for the Voice's signal to shout my discovery of the death ray. I sensed its use was limited by its terrifying power. To eliminate several people in order to save one person would defeat its purpose.

I used the after-dinner silence to make my announcement: "Political prisoners, the miraculous Machine," my cry sounded loud and clear, "can protect you with its death-ray."

I stopped. Nameless didn't jump to wrap his tentacle-like arms around me. The door did not swing open.

"I warn the guards. Do not dare step across the threshold... " I became increasingly more brave.

No answer... no movement. Did they know about the existence of the Machine?

"Do not dare enter my cell!"

No one moved.

I yelled without reprisal. How was that possible? Were they afraid?

Next morning, I tried the power of the ray again. When the clumsy guard who had never hurt me, came to hand in the water buckets, I yelled at him: "Don't step into the cell... If you cross the threshold the ray might kill you."

He stayed outside and waved at Nameless to take the water from him.

Was it true the Voice could punish with such severity? Had I transgressed the limits of Its permission? Had I abused Its power?

A sergeant I had not seen previously tried to enter. I warned him also. He stopped short at the door, hesitated, then entered anyway.

He didn't fall down, the death-ray did not kill him, but he did not hit me either.

"Don't shout," he advised me. "I don't want to hurt you, I only brought you books if you want them."

"I want to see the prosecutor, not books. For months I have been kept among convicts. Why?"

"I can't answer that question," he shrugged. "I can only exchange your books."

I could hardly wait for him to leave, so I could return to my conversation with the Voice.

As soon as I proclaimed the death-ray, they stopped torturing me;

they left me alone even when I shouted the threatening message of the death-ray into the jail's silent night.

I had no other explanation.

THE VOICE IS NO MORE

The clinking of the breakfast dishes promised nothing new. Light blinked through the thin slits in the planks of the cell's boarded up window. This impenetrable "window" twisted the reason for its existence. Unlike other windows, it served only to shut out the light and noise of the outside world.

"It's been like that for months," the Voice joined my thoughts. "You just didn't notice."

"I couldn't have cared less."

"Do you think the rest of the windows are like that?"

I couldn't answer: I had no way of peeking into the other cells. I lived like a clam in its thick, assigned shell.

"What would you think," It asked with a weakened sound, "if I left you?"

"It's happened before that you left me for a long time."

"But, if I left you... forever!"

My heart throbbed so hard it seemed to break in two.

"Would you really leave me?" I stammered.

"Yes... forever!"

I tried not to think of the implications of this announcement. Nothing was solved yet. I was marking time in irons, among convicts, in the company of a nameless stool-pigeon, behind a boarded up window. What will I do all by myself? I begged. Who will provide me with advice? Who will protect me? The Voice led me towards truth, promised me freedom, escape. It was my second self who was much better than I was, It calmed my fears and my enthusiasms, It dictated my attempts to give signs of life.

"How can you do this to me?" my will to survive screamed.

I barely heard Its answer: "I will leave you."

What had I done to evoke this? Where did I go wrong? Had I missed one of Its advises? Was I complaining about Its help, having had doubts about Its effectiveness? Was I actually doubting Its very existence?

"Impossible!" My cry desperately called for the Voice that had become the mainstay of my isolated prison life. I clung to It now like a drowning man to a plank. "You have existed and you will exist. You protect and guide me. You gave me orders and I followed. You saved me."

163

No answer came to my inner cry. I bit my lips so hard I tasted blood.

It occurred to me: should the Voice leave me unexpectedly in this chaos, when I still so badly needed It, maybe It had never existed...

The mere possibility of the Voice's departure was a madman's terrifying nightmare for me.

If the Voice never existed, then neither did the miraculous Machine. The entire technological structure, with its modern spectacle, built to lead humanity towards truth, justice and freedom, would collapse.

But, if there was no Voice, no Machine, then how had I foreseen the innumerable episodes that materialized exactly as I had predicted them?

The Voice must have been real. Its terrifying announcements, surprising predictions, the ability to read people's minds proved Its existence. Other proofs were prophecies that materialized such as: the guard will open the peep-hole, he will beat my head with the billy club, the doctor will come, he will give me an injection, they will take me into the shower, I will change prisons, and all of the other tiny predictions that were explicable only through Its existence.

It told me the rank of "Sir," Leather-cap, and the fish-eyed doctor's leading position. It told me everything,... everything I needed to know... Without the Voice, all of this would have been impossible.

One terrifying thought chased the other: if there was no Voice then I, too, was nothing. I was a speck of dust, dropped into the desert of evil. The film, the tape of our fate, the proof of our truth and justice disappeared to nothingness! No... I refused to believe it... No... it couldn't be!

"But,... what if it still was true?"

I heard a breeze-like inkling; a weak, cowardly SOMETHING that may have been the Voice, or just the echo of my own doubts. Was it an awakening to my hellish fate; a return to gray reality?

If the Voice had never existed, if it was a mere figment of my imagination, my hallucinations, then.. without a doubt I must have been crazy... a true madman!

It didn't matter how they made me crazy, what power of poison swept me into the nether world of madness, the fact remained; if there was no Voice, my subconscious took over and ruled my conscious world for months. It happened in exactly the same way I had described the role of the subconscious ego to the AVH during that time when "telling the truth" motivated and persecuted me.

I turned my head, twisted and searched radar-like to find the ray, wave, oscillation or fragment of sound beamed towards me through ether. I often managed to find the Voice like that.

It will appear! It would happen like it did the first time, when the Voice crept beside me in that first dreadful moment. When after my great confession fear gripped me and doubt rose in my heart, the Voice dispersed the conviction that I had been trapped.

Would It leave me now? Would my cry for help remain unanswered?

Suddenly, as if a butterfly's wings stirred the air, a tiny, almost inaudible buzz answered. It sounded like the ocean's song in a shell when held to the ear, bringing the message of infinity. This sound reminded me of the music of the waterpipes, that terrifying choir in the apocalyptic hours in the underground cell.

"I am leaving... I am leaving... FOREVER!... FOREVER!" It repeated, weakly droning.

The sound faded away. Silence enveloped me.

The whispered parting words must have been figments of my imagination. If there was no Voice, It could not have said good-bye to me. How could something depart that never existed?

It was finished. No more Voice. I had to accept the fact: I had conducted endless discussions with my own imagination. The Machine and the Voice had never existed.

I was left hopelessly alone.

My reality was this cell with its blind window, where Nameless stared at me without a word. He watched me, according to his orders, but he knew nothing about my inner struggle. I irretrievably lost the battle of truth. Reality took the place of truth.

* * *

Nameless' hostile presence increased my sense of loneliness. I had to get used to it. After my long alliance with the Voice, who ruled above me, guided me and was supreme, my inner resources seemed inadequate.

I took inventory of solid facts. I was in a huge prison complex, completely isolated from the outside world. I had received treatment from doctors who gave me injections, called me a madman, and put me in a straitjacket. The authorities gave me Nameless as a cell-mate and tortured me for pleasure.

Even if the Voice had not existed, It was right. Had my signs of life, given at Its command, saved my life? Only the Voice could have solved this riddle, but It was no more.

I felt at the mercy of the system. This feeling was no easier to cope with than the Voice's wild orders and the following tortures. I continued to be a hidden, nameless number in the power of madmen. My sense of equality with them lasted only as long as I, too, was a madman.

I waved away my thoughts. Nameless became aware of my agitation. He put down his book and stared at me. I waited impatiently for the guard to take him for his walk. I wanted to be alone to continue my spiritual spring cleaning.

His walk was too short. Nameless returned in a bad mood. He huddled on his bed as if he expected something.

Half an hour later the guard came for him, yelling: "Get your stuff! Everything!"

He was out on the corridor in no time at all. The cell door slammed shut. The guard's felt boots marched next to Nameless' shuffle.

When the guard returned, he winked at me saying, "I guess you won't be mourning for him! He's gone for good. You'll be left alone."

His friendly behavior made me brave: "What month is it, can you tell me?"

"March. March, 1953."[1]

This date was very important to me. I regained control of my mind, but I had lost the Voice forever.

---

[1] Stalin died March 5, 1953.

CHANGE

End of March, 1953

I turned to my allotted reading material with increasing interest. Yesterday the librarian let me keep four of ten books.

I started with Stalin's "The Questions of Leninism." He openly declared to the world: "The people's democracy is the equivalent of the dictatorship of the proletariat," which in turn was "the system of lawless force."

My second book described the "Rajk trial." The picture I formed of him based on newspaper reports at the time was of a true Communist presented by the system as a Western spy. The book confirmed my opinions.

"Behind the Surgeon's Mask" contained interesting revelations. The short stories were taken from a psychiatrist's confessions and psychiatric analyses, as well as the possible influence of certain medications. The book gave intriguing explanations and solutions to my connections with the Voice.

I greedily absorbed the text. It was public knowledge that drugs and poisons can disturb the balance of our inner world. This book ascertained my suspicion: the "soup" at AVH's Veszprem prison served this purpose in my case.

The fourth book, which dealt with the "Reichstag" trial, described the accused being treated with chemicals. The Soviets have only "perfected" the Nazi's psychiatric experiments.

Based on this knowledge, my own destiny and future political trial logically unfolded in my mind. When my friends and I have to stand trial, I will have to defend our cause. My words will no longer be dictated by the Voice, but will reflect the conscious self-defense of a lawyer, of the counsel for the defense, a professional decision, and the mandatory defense of the accused.

My work, a considerable legal task, was cut out for me.

Truth was as important as the Voice had taught me throughout the past months. If the Voice merely brought my subconscious, my true identity, to the surface of my conscious, then I had to follow the dictates of my subconscious even when sober. The seed of Its teaching stayed with me.

"How are you doing, Mr. Tottosy?"

My cell door stood wide open. The stump-eared major led a troop consisting of a lieutenant, a second lieutenant and three sergeants.

"Fine, thanks," I muttered.

He stepped to the blind window.

"Can't you open this window?" he asked the sergeant as if he had discovered something entirely new. The sergeant, surprised by the question, stammered his response.

"Indeed, no Comrade Major!" he answered obediently. The "indeed" sounded strange, but the major, as a good actor, just shook his head and said:

"Well... well... and they don't even take you for a walk?"

"No, sir. I have not breathed fresh air or seen the sun in eight months."

"We'll have to change that. From now on you will go for walks twice a day. And you will get a better cell."

He looked around, searching for something.

"Do you smoke?"

"No."

He fished out a handful of fine cigarettes from his jacket pocket and placed it on my bed.

"It doesn't matter. You can smoke them whenever you are in the mood."

I had the feeling he was not only embarrassed, he wanted to make reparations.

Why? Had something changed in here, or on the outside?[1]

Certainly the behavior of everyone had changed. Did all of these changes serve as psychological preparation for the trial? Did my captors want to seem more benevolent, so I would forget the past?

A few hours after the departure of the major, they led me to a new cell. The clean room with two beds, on the main floor, radiated a different atmosphere. The lukewarm spring sun poured into the room through the open window and red geraniums bloomed on the windowsill. Bees buzzed around the flowers.

I breathed in the thin air, all the way down, to the bottom of my soul. My senses reeled, intoxicated with the long forgotten smell of life.

* * *

---

[1] After Stalin's death, at the influence of the Soviet Union, Hungary changed its mode of torture. The powerful and their servants became alarmed by the smell of the torture chambers and opened their doors. The doctors who administered poisons and their special troops were frightened when Beria's fate became common knowledge. The turn of the Kremlin's destiny made the terror-apparatus think.

My new spiritual delicacies, books, lay on the snow white linen in the caressing sun. Books and sunshine — the ecstasy of the moment fired me with enthusiasm. I felt the same gratitude that a person on death row feels when a humane executioner brings him a bowl of hot soup before the execution.

How easy it was to buy human gratitude! Why should I be thankful to those wardens who kept me here secretly in violation of the law, of my human rights; who tossed me from cell to cell for unknown reasons? I didn't even understand why this new development took place.

The guard took me for my walk alone.

I had heard the shuffling of the other prisoners' feet in the gallery often, as they stampeded for their walk. I became so accustomed to the fact that, on account of my secret mission, I was not one of them, I had never even asked myself why they neglected to take me. I did not envy the other prisoners: I had no desire to trade places with them.

I became acquainted with the huge, spiritless yard. Its deserted, pebbled terrain stretched between the enormous wings of the buildings.

I scrutinized my guard who dragged his feet a few steps behind me. I remembered him: he was the palefaced, rankless young man, who accompanied my torture squad several times, but never hurt me. He always stayed a few steps behind them and never budged, even when the gypsy second lieutenant pulled the straps of my straitjacket tighter, or held my nose. Now he stepped up to walk beside me:

"Do you remember me?" he whispered.

Surprised, I slowed my pace.

"Please, don't slow down, Mr. Attorney, sir, keep moving."

I continued in my former rhythm.

"Do you remember me?" he repeated.

"Yes."

"I saw what they did to you. It must have been terrible. Do you remember everything?"

"Everything!"

"Then you must remember I never hurt you."

"You were a good man."

I couldn't see his face, but I sensed he expected this answer.

"The tortures are over," he whispered confidentially.

He let me walk for more than half an hour.

"Come!" he finally stopped me. "Walk time was over quite a while ago."

This boy was honest. My future did not interest him, he wanted to know what I remembered about him. Was he afraid of something?

In the solitude of my cell, questions flooded me: what had changed? Were they preparing for something? What did all this so called good-will hide?

I tried to bury myself in books.

A few days later they took me to the upstairs interrogation room. The guard whispered: "They will question you." I looked at him with surprised suspicion. In the past, none of them ever revealed what would happen to me next.

He asked me to sit down in the empty room.

"Sir," my old interrogator, entered in a well-tailored AVH uniform. My eyes glanced at his gold epaulets. He had the rank of first lieutenant. I fully expected the Voice to chime in: "See, I told you so!"

Silence stretched between us, the Voice did not show up. I had to realize I must have simply guessed his rank previously.

"How do you feel?" he asked.

"Fine, thank you."

He did not spread any papers on his table as was his custom. He had no pen or pencil with him.

"Do they take you for a walk regularly?" he scrutinized me.

"Yes."

"Are you content with your new cell?"

"Yes."

"Do you receive books and cigarettes?"

"I get books, but I don't smoke."

Their cigarette-mania angered me. They thought they could buy any prisoner for three cigarettes.

"We are finished with your case," he said in a measured tone. "You may well leave here soon."

I did not ask him what that meant. To me this was a warning for a change. What would come after a window with geraniums?

"I know many unusual things happened to you," he started. His voice sounded insecure. I waited for his explanation curiously.

"You must recognize though, you too behaved in an unusual manner. You rebelled, we had to curb you. However, as a lawyer... you must know... "

He stopped. He looked me up and down meaningfully.

"Before as well as after sentencing, at all times, you remain in the hands of the authorities."

The "authorities," the omnipotent AVH, stood above the government, the state, the ministers, the Party secretaries. It was not a "state within the state," but a "state above the state." Their instruments were investigation, tortures, fabricated "court sentences," "putting in irons," and "settling under their own jurisdiction."[2]

---

[2]After 1945 the Communist Party immediately monopolized the security police. Its first name was the "state security department" — the initials of which were AVO in

His voice continued, not threatening, rather self-confidently.

"I hope you also know," he looked up at me, "your fate in front of the judge will depend on... " he searched for the right word. "It will depend on what kind of relations you had with us. Don't even think of talking about anything not closely related to your case. You know how easily we can handle those who rebel... "

I understood his threat. He often asked me: "Why are you rebelling?", when I stood before him numb, weakened by the tortures of the underground prison. Did he want to remind me of that? To forget all my revolts? How about the doctors, the injections, the showers — did they use them as punishments also?

I did not point out his contradictions. I was no longer crazy. Only they remained madmen. It would be foolish to argue with madmen, especially when they held so much power in their hands.

His visible insecurity made me feel the more secure.

"I will hold up my confessions, lieutenant," I tried to comfort him, "and I will not add anything to them."

"We expect this from you. Even if unusual things did happen to you, you must forget them. Do you understand?"

"I understand."

We both understood.

"Behave intelligently," he said as we parted after the guard had appeared, summoned by the secret bell.

Two or three quiet weeks followed.

The guards treated me politely, I could choose my own books, they gave me as much prison food as I wanted. Occasionally a butterfly strayed in my window, then returned to freedom when it found its way out.

One day while I followed the tracks of one of these delightful creatures, a huge fly flew into my ear. I had never experienced anything like that before. The crazed scratching of the fly against my eardrum was unbearable. I yelled for help at the top of my lungs. My desperate cries for help disturbed the silence of the cells. The guards had every right to think I was staging another mad scene.

Two of them ran in. I explained my problem with my head pressed to the ground. The clever inventiveness of these boys, brought up in the country, surprised me. My law degree gave me no help when confronted with the need to chase a crazed fly out of my ear. One of the

---

Hungarian, of the Ministry of the Interior. On September 6, 1948, the "authority for state security", AVH, was formed by order of the Ministry of the Interior, though most of the public continued to call it AVO.

December 28, 1949, brought a new change. By order of the Council of Ministers the AVH was reorganized. According to this, the AVH reported directly to the Council of Ministers and had an entirely separate budget. Its officers, from lieutenant colonel up, were appointed by the Presidential Council at the recommendation of the Council of Ministers.

sergeants, however, knew just what to do. He ran away and returned in a few seconds with a pitcher of water.

"Turn your ear to me!" he said and performed a perfect "surgery."

Three days later the commander of the jail, the stump-eared major came for another courtesy visit. Again two higher and two lower ranking officers followed him.

After the customary "how are you's" he examined my books to show his benevolent interest. Surprised, he lifted Stalin's "Questions of Leninism."

"You read such stuff, too?" he asked astounded. He apparently cound not believe his eyes.

"Why not, major? I found many interesting things in it."

The prison commander of the "system of lawless force" had a hard time understanding: a good political strategy involves an intimate knowledge of the opponent's theories.

He put the book back down onto the bed.

"Let me know if you have any wishes."

"I have one, Major."

"Yes?"

"I would like to send a message to my family."

My wish surprised him.

"I will talk to your investigator. But, I know, as long as your case is being investigated this would be entirely impossible."

I knew, everyone knew: prisoners of cases with secret files marked "00" lived in a separate world. For them there was no law to protect them, no counsel for the defense, and no family.[3]

At this moment I felt stronger than all of their power put together.

Lies built the society of madmen, such a rule of force stood on shifting sands. It was only a matter of time: four years, ten, fifty, and the building would collapse. Our entire lives — a whole generation — might pass before it happened, but ultimately it would collapse.

---

[3] The filing system of the cases marked "00" was introduced by the system in 1949-50. Such cases were always political. they received entirely separate, secret office treatment. The Office of Criminal Justice — mostly the Marko Street Court — was not allowed to give any kind of information to any lawyer about those files. This system constituted a grave violation of the traditional rights of the defendant.

Prisoners arrested and held by the AVH were not allowed to have visitors, neither lawyer nor family. Their fates were entirely unknown, just as their places of imprisonment. They did not receive a bill of indictment as a rule, they could only be defended by those lawyers included on the AVH's list of counsels for the defense, and appointed by them. In most cases these appointed lawyers were the AVH's confidants and spies.

THE ALIBI

"Change your clothes!" the guard handed me my moldy, ragged, and bloodstained civilian clothes.

Hope swayed me. I saw it clearly: I will not be discharged, but there will be a decisive change in my fate.

"They are taking you!" Then he added: "Maybe they'll release you." Had they lied to him? Or did he want to console me?

I sat alone in a locked paddy wagon as it sped through town.

After a ride of about three-quarters of an hour, they led me to a new cell, amidst unknown buildings and a jungle of barracks. A rude man in prison-garb, the person on duty, fed me and ordered me around as if he were in charge of the entire prison.

At any rate, it seemed like a mighty strange way to bring someone to court. The barracks couldn't possibly be a prison, let alone an AVH investigative unit or a court. What in the world were they, then?

My investigator let me know that the AVH had concluded my investigation. Where could my partners be? When were they caught in the diabolical net the AVH wove around us in these past months?

If the authorities were preparing — so was I.

My thoughts dwelt on the one chance I would get in court. Unlike Cardinal Mindszenty and the rest, I will talk when the judge asks me at the end of the trial if I have any last words to bring up in my defense. I laid out my plans in my small cell.

I decided not to talk about the treatment I had received. No one would believe it! No illegal treatment against my person could be the subject of a "conspiracy trial." However, I wanted to tell the world how those in control of the AVH conspired, how they organized and carried out their plot against the Hungarian people!

In our case we were merely conspiring against their power: against lawlessness, against inhumanity, and against torture.

The Universal Declaration of Human Rights permits individuals to rise up against "tyranny," considering this kind of revolt as self-defense, applied in dire emergency. We acted in self-defense!

We never thought of force. We made plans for jovial bourgeois lives, we didn't forge plans involving arms, blood, and sacrifice.

The great majority of organizations in Hungary — whether we call them conspiracies or not — never dream of toppling the regime by force. Almost all of them consist of peaceful conversations, weaving dreams of a democratic transformation. Social and political democracy constitute the dreams of those who are being secretly tried and hanged or sentenced to long years of imprisonment as "conspirators."

I, as the counsel for the defense, had to organize all of this material. The canvas of my mind was my only tool; I drafted a speech which became a prosecutor's accusation. It might be my last one — after it they would definitely hang me. Despite this certain knowledge, I decided to go ahead with it — in case I managed to avoid manipulation, psychiatric treatment, the injection, and retained control of my senses, — that is, if I still possessed all my faculties by the time of our trial. My defense-turned-into-indictment could materialize only if the authorities decided to blow up our case into a showcase trial; if they needed to flaunt their power again after the trials of Mindszenty, Rajk and Grosz.

Days and weeks had passed. The Voice did not return.

If fate willed me to play this role to the bitter end, I wanted to play it well. In the life of a lawyer there was no greater or a more majestic moment than to deliver a good defense. I remembered the driving force that arose from knowing that the emotional influence of my arguments would decide the fate of a man. Even today I felt in my blood the hopes of the accused, I saw the trust in his eyes, the attention of the council, the vexation of the prosecutor and his secret admiration, the tense excitement of the audience.

My assigned counsel for the defense could not be anyone but a representative of the AVH and consequently would be able to say only what they allowed him. Therefore I would defend my partners and myself, and through our case, the entire Hungarian nation.

I paced my cell with tiny steps. The summer heat lured my desire to live. I felt the outside world close to me; if I could just stretch out my arm and touch it! I knew free people lived beyond my open window. They went on excursions, they walked on the quays of the Danube, and they swam and went boating in its waters.

I stood on my tiptoes to see a bigger chunk of sky. The clear, cloudless radiant opal embraced Budapest. Maybe it was Sunday. It reminded me of the many times when I trusted myself to the majestic Danube's flow along with the other thousands of "drifters." The river carried its many travelers with peaceful serenity. Its surface mirrored the sky.

* * *

In the morning sunshine, hiding behind the cell window I practiced my great defense for the second time that day, according to the daily routine I set for myself.

I placed my jacket on the bed. The July sun warmed my cell.

Two guards came to retrieve me: "Come," the higher ranked one beckoned.

He led me through zig-zagging corridors to a room. I stopped short in front of the door because close to twenty pairs of eyes stared at me through the open door.

These were not the well-groomed troops of AVH guards I faced before. These fallen-faced, unshaven, badly dressed people had to be prisoners like myself.

"Good morning, gentlemen!" I tried to thaw the ice-cold atmosphere of our mutual surprise. "Where am I?"

They stood as stiffly as wax figurines. One of them, a stubble-faced man of about fifty stepped towards me.

"You are in Kistarcsa, a concentration camp," he answered, still in an ice-cold tone.

"Good God," I blurted in surprise, "What am I doing here?"

"Probably, whatever all of us are!" my reaction brought a smile to his face.

This broke the ice and others started to approach me.

The stubble-chinned man shook my hand and said his name, but I could not understand it, except that he was a general. This friendly prison-protocol was new to me and I stumbled in introducing myself. I also told them I was a lawyer from Budapest.

"And, being a lawyer, you still didn't know where they brought you?" the general asked.

"Indeed I didn't. Besides, the law books do not describe Kistarcsa anywhere. And unfortunately, law plays a mighty small role in this country."

He smiled again, but I did not know whether or not his distrust dissolved completely.

"You are the first living beings I could call human whom I have seen in a year," I continued my explanation.

"How come?" he pulled up his eyebrow.

"The AVH arrested me more than a year ago. They isolated me from the world the entire time."

Immediately a circle gathered around me. They examined me like a flock of sparrows would a crow that strayed into their midst.

"You mean the AVH held you for a year?" the general asked.

"Yes."

"Where?"

"First at the Veszprem AVH. From there they brought me to Budapest to an underground dungeon. I have no idea where that could have been. Then they took me to a huge prison building, but I never saw that one before either. For the past two months they had kept me here."

"You are a lawyer and you were not familiar with the prisons?"

"Only prisoners know the jails from the inside. The lawyer gets stuck at the railing where he talks with his clients. And you? Did the AVH hold you also?"

"Since they had returned us from the Soviet Union where we had been since the end of the war. Some of us stayed in prisoner of war camps, others in prisons. A miracle brought us back home."

"What miracle?"

"Stalin died in March."

I bit my lips. In March... exactly six months after October, when the Voice prophesied he would die.

"Is everything all right?" the general asked, as if he guessed my thoughts were on a different track. "You didn't know about it?"

"No... but I sensed it."

"The whole world cheered the news. There must have been great changes within the Kremlin, because unthinkable changes have happened here in Hungary. Imre Nagy took over from Rakosi..."

"Imre Nagy?"

"The new Soviet leaders put their trust in him. Everyone knew: even though he, too, was a Moscovite newcomer, he was much more popular. He announced a new program and brought with him a much freer atmosphere."

"Freer atmosphere?... Inasmuch as... ?"

"He disbanded the concentration camps, let the 'internal exiles,' you know, the people deported in 1951, go home. He returned us from the Soviet Union where they wanted to make us die like dogs. Allegedly, the AVH stopped its usual methods of torture. The bloodhounds are afraid that Beria's fate might become theirs."

"What happened to Beria?"

"He was put aside. Which is not such big news because from among his predecessors, Djerzhinsky was the only one who avoided violent death. Allegedly, the Soviets discontinued torture as well."

These words opened a whole new world for me. They answered some of my questions, they explained the better treatment, the fear and caution of the AVH.

"And you? Why are you here after being prisoners of war?" I couldn't wait to hear.

The general twitched his mouth.

"Hungarian fate is not all it's drummed up to be. Rakosi and the AVH still remain in the background. They are merely a bit more cautious; they got scared. They brought us here to be screened. Whoever is guilty will be put in jail.

"You will see a prosecutor?"

"Supposedly, we are here waiting for interrogation by a prosecutor. But don't get your hopes up too high! It's still the same system, only the methods have changed."

As if on cue, the guard came for me. Drunk by the impact of the extraordinary news, I staggered after him. These few minutes had changed my world. I finally could breathe the fresh air freely, having had to suck in my sustenance from under a bell jar for a long time.

A solitary desk stood in the room where the guard pushed me. A rusty-haired, long-faced civilian showed me to a chair and bade me to sit down.

If the disappearance of the Voice had left me feeling lonely and weaker, the news I just heard filled me with self-confidence.

"I'd like to know who you are?" I asked with more courage than I thought I had in me.

The civilian looked up at the unexpected tone.

"I am a state prosecutor. You will have a hearing."

My temporary room-mates told the truth. Finally, after a year, I was sitting in front of a state prosecutor. This man who distractedly leafed through his papers, right here, in front of me, was the protector of law.

"You were interrogated several times by the AVH, weren't you?" he looked up at me.

"I was. However, I would like to ask you to register my protest: after more than one year, this is the first time they let me talk to a prosecutor."

"This is not my concern," he shrugged.

Typical answer; the highest prosecuting power indifferently shrugs off my complaint, claiming illegal handling of prisoners is not his concern. Whose then?

He looked at my file as if nothing else existed for him. He had to produce an indictment out of that. The file also managed to completely hide from him the person involved.

"But, please... Mr. Prosecutor," I said, reddened by anger.

He interrupted me: "I am warning you. Here — I am the only one asking questions."

That brought me to my senses. Even if Stalin's death had shaken the world, the question still remained whether or not it shook the power of the Hungarian state prosecutor. Any heroism, any protest would be plain stupidity. I understood I had to suppress all kinds of further protests.

"Do you uphold your confessions made to the AVH?" the prosecutor got straight to his point. "I will not go into details because we will still interrogate you."

"I uphold them."

"Without any changes?"

"Yes."

"Soon you will get away from here," he said, then to the guard: "You can take him now."

Another guard took me back to the loneliness of my cell. The elixirs of the morning spread through my whole body. I remembered the events of the past months: the stump-eared prison commander's sudden kindness, the change in my treatment by the AVH guards, and the disappearance of the doctors. It all made sense now.

Small Hungary can only do what Moscow wills. If the Soviets loosen the handcuffs of the prisoners, if they put aside the highest inquisitors, then that method has to be followed by their satellites.

What mattered to me most was that I finally stood in front of a prosecutor. This was the first legal step after an entire year — the first normal step taken inside the society of madmen.

I could see clearly now why they brought me to the concentration camp at Kistarcsa. They wanted to legalize that infamous year during which they held me in the AVH prisons illegally. To justify their actions, they suddenly had to comply with formalities of the law — because of the Kremlin's will.

Finally I became a living being, a true registry number, and an existing "00" file.

SHOWCASE TRIAL?

About two weeks passed before they transferred me again. This time the paddy wagon stopped in front of a well-known building. The red brick palace served at one time as the District Court of Pest and Vicinity, now it belonged to the AVH.

They transformed the whole building: the conference rooms and judicial chambers became cells and interrogation rooms. The wide corridors of the courthouse preserved their cold respectability, but the building no longer housed justice.

"Small courts... enormous prisons, the characteristics of a totalitarian dictatorship," I kept repeating the words of my intended defense.

My new cell had two beds with clean sheets. The food turned out to be acceptable. I had not even spent a whole week alone when the guard brought a slim, young prisoner who introduced himself as Geza P., seminarian. He had returned from the West... with an assignment.

They accused him of spying, even though the information he gathered was extremely inconsequential. His assignment was more childish than dangerous, but, to his great misfortune, they found a revolver on him. The young seminarian, an enthusiastic, brave Hungarian, tried to accomplish a stupid and heartless mission for those who sent him. What kind of a fool entrusted him with a revolver he could not even use? He didn't say and I didn't ask. Only a few months ago his predecessors in similar crimes were sentenced with the speed of lightning and immediately hanged.

"Times have changed," he said. "The rigor of the AVH relaxed. They haven't touched me." He proved to be a great source of information.

"What if you don't have a showcase trial?" he stopped me one day during our walk, while I rehearsed my talk over and over.

"If I don't have a showcase trial?" I repeated the question. "I won't even open my mouth."

"It doesn't make sense to make more trouble for yourself. They may even..." he bit his tongue. He did not want to finish his sentence.

"... they may even hang you."

The guard interrupted our conversation.

In the interrogation room, "Sir" sat in civilian clothes. A pockmark-faced stranger stood beside him. They scrutinized me without words.

"We are finished with your case," said "Sir," pointing to a chair. "A week ago we arrested your partners."

He watched my face when he announced they had waited a whole year to arrest my partners.

"What kind of punishment do you expect?" he asked when the silence became oppressive.

"I have no idea," my voice shook with fear. "Will it be a showcase trial?"

"What is a showcase trial?" he groaned.

"I mean — public hearing?"

"That I understand," he was willing to let my slip go. "That remains to be seen. That depends on many things. However, you know, if you get more than 10 years, it may as well be a death sentence."

"I know," I whispered.

"Comrade colonel here," he looked at the civilian standing beside him, "would like to have a word with you."

The civilian stepped forward to give more emphasis to the introduction.

"I have seen your children's pictures," he said confidentially. "I bet you are dying to see them as soon as possible."

"Yes."

"Sir" took over from there. "Comrade colonel gave me permission to explain to you a solution for a speedy release... "

I thought I hadn't heard well. First they threatened me with 10 years, then they lured me with the possibility of a speedy discharge?

"**We know you have suffered,**" he continued. Of course, **you are the cause of that to a certain extent because you kept rebelling.** However, we know, even though you are an enemy of proletarian power, you love your country."

"That is true."

"What would happen if you told the court you spent this past year in the West, in a refugee camp near Vienna. You became disillusioned with the Western world and you came home because you loved your country."

I understood all.

They wanted to make my illegal year vanish. They wanted to erase all traces of my "madness." They didn't care about the thousands who heard my name shouted in the night, who knew I had been in Hungary during that past year. They needed my "confession"! Who would doubt my words if I, myself, told of returning home from abroad. Would this false confession buy a speedy release?

"Look," he interrupted my inner struggle, "if you accept this confession, the authorities promise: you will be let off with an 18 month sentence."

Good God! Was escape this near? I merely had to sign a few supplementary lines in my report? Who would be hurt by it? My partners were arrested only recently: I might even be able to help them.

But, what if they lied? If, instead of 18 months I would get 12 years, or even death. They had promised Rajk a Crimean vacation and then hanged him.

The temptation was tremendous. My practical mind, my first instinct of self-interest stood in opposition with an extremely strong, crazed inner defiance. The "conscience-machine," activated in me by the Voice, would not let me act for my own interests.

The truth of my prepared defense speech supported the seed of my madness — that stubborn, illogical thing that forced me to tell the truth. For a year I struggled for truth with the help of the Voice, and now I would throw away my achievement, in exchange of this false-truth?

"Colonel, sir," I formed my inner struggle into words, "the AVH always asked for the truth from me."

Did I bring this up in defense, or did I want to prove myself? I wanted to bring up their contradictions so they had to pronounce the judgement. Why should I have to choose between freedom and truth — when both are sacred? Which comes out a winner in this struggle: the instinct for life or spiritual force?

"That is true," the colonel conceded with a sour face. "We want truth about everything you did. However, it could easily have happened that you escaped... "

"But it didn't," I retorted.

"Who cares about that today? We cannot turn back the hands of time and redo things in a different way. Our proposition is first of all for your own good, it would give you back your freedom. You've gone through 'quite a todo,' already... "

That phrase, 'quite a todo', fired my blood. For him, for the authorities, to chase people into madness, to make their brains numb with poison, the tortures, the bloody incidents of tying down people, and to put them in irons was: "quite a todo."

"Colonel, sir," I asked, lobster-red, "may I ask something?"

"Ask," he nodded with his head angrily.

"If the system before the war would have made a similar suggestion to a true Communist," I spit the words out, "do you think he would have accepted the offer?"

They looked at each other shocked, but none of them answered.

"I am certain he wouldn't have!" I continued, determined. "You always demanded the truth from me. I will give you that truth, I will confess the truth, but without any changes or additions."

They understood.

"All right," the colonel waved away the whole thing with his hand. "Mad man!" my interrogator hissed. "You remain a madman!"

Behind closed doors, the "anti-government organizational" case of myself and ten friends came to trial.

Our trail did not become a "showcase."

I never again saw an investigator, or the state prosecutor. In November of 1953 they transferred me — alone — to the Marko Street Court where they kept me with the political prisoners.

On January 14, 1954 — eighteen months after my arrest — I was finally tried by the Jonas council of the Budapest Court.[1] Jonas, the Chief Justice in charge of political cases of the Hungarian criminal system, announced his judgement within a few hours of the trial that was closed to the public.

He sentenced me to 12 years, which the AVH qualified as "equivalent to death."

Jonas, the presiding judge, knew my file well.

He acted in a dry, correct way, true to the system, having received his instructions from the AVH ahead of time. No outside participant disturbed the dread silence of the closed trial. The two investigators in the back of the chambers could not be considered outsiders as they were the true representatives of the judicial power. The phantom of the showcase trials disappeared in the windstorm that shook the Kremlin walls and the whole Communist world. The terror apparatus of Hungary, though slowed, continued to turn its wheels. Jonas, the presiding judge, seemed to feel the wind too.

He hurried his questions like someone who could not wait to finish the case. He hurried, — although he did not see it yet — towards the death already knocking at his door. On November 1, 1956, driven by fear of revenge by those he condemned, he turned on the gas and died.

The prosecutor was the rusty-haired one who questioned me at Kistarcsa. He opened his indictment by saying: "... after the Mindszenty and Grosz trials, as a result of a new attack by clerical reactionaries, this conspiracy may be regarded as the third Mindszenty trial."

He represented the AVH correctly. He did not ask for death, only for a strict sentence.

My counsel for the defense was appointed by the court, as was the custom in "00" cases. I had never received a bill of indictment in my case, so my counsel did not have to discuss it with me in a legal hearing either. He only had to ask the AVH's opinion.

---

[1] I knew Jonas, the presiding judge, very well, when he judged ordinary cases. He became the chief justice in charge of the "00" political cases only after my arrest. He proved to be a sharp-minded, pedantic cog in the apparatus of the dictatorship.

I felt honored by the person of the counsel for the defense. He was none other than Istvan Nagy, the Chief Prosecutor of the Bar Association of Budapest, the President of the Association of Hungarian Jurists, the innermost confident of the AVH, a bosom-buddy of the Party aristocracy, and the first man in the justice machinery of Stalin.[2]

He, too, was "correct." He refrained from accusing me with any more than the prosecutor had.

That was the last time I saw him. Did he sense what fate had in store for him? During the 1956 revolution, allegedly on November 1st, a Budapest attorney beat him to death.

With this much "correct" help the judicial council could only bring a "correct" judgement. In the midst of Imre Nagy's period of relaxation, they handed down close to a hundred years of sentences for the 10 of us. Only the Kremlin's order for thaw saved us from death sentences.

The "showcase trial" did not materialize, but after several years of imprisonment, plenty of surprises and new investigations concerning an invented "conspiracy," something much more majestic came instead: the Hungarian people's showcase trial and judgement of the system ruling them. In 1956 the Hungarian people condemned to death the Jonases, the Istvan Nagy's, the investigators... THE SOCIETY OF MADMEN.

---

[2] I also knew Istvan Nagy well. In 1951, prior to my arrest, he called me to his office at the Bar Association and after my threat-filled hearing he parted with these words: "You are one of our top young lawyers. Unfortunately, you are also one of the leading figures of the clerical reactionary forces. You are our enemy. We will destroy you."

EPILOGUE

Copenhagen, May 29, 1982

Dr. Ernest Tottosy
3 Avenue Lambeau
1200 Bruzelles

My dear Friend,

    I was out of town and that prevented me from answering your letter of May 8th any sooner. I am sorry to hear you suffer from the same illness I do; I receive three shots a week for my heart problems and soon I will undergo heart surgery — if it has any sense at all. Life treated both of us roughly — now we have to pay for it.
    I have no newspaper clippings and to my knowledge there were no other articles. I cannot get to the archives in the Royal Library here because the newspaper archives are in the middle of moving. They will be closed for at least six months. Later I hope to send you some material. After all, you will not be able to write your book with the speed of lightning anyway.
    I have to clarify my role in connection with your case. I was not the one who wanted to help you across the Austrian border. I intended to escape with you. Our guide would have been Gabor Molnar. I was merely his helper. I was drafted in the Army, and sent to Petfurdo. Save for that I would have been arrested, along with you. As it happened they arrested me only after I served my three months in the Army, on the day of my discharge: September 19, 1952. The same day they confronted us in Veszprem.
    I made Molnar's acquaintance at work in 1947. At that time I was the foreign affairs editor of the newspaper published by Barankovics's Democratic People's Party. Barankovics escaped in 1949 and left the editorial staff in the claws of the AVH. After a short time in jail, I was allowed to go home, but they often searched my apartment. I kept in contact with Molnar. I had no means of supporting myself and I was under constant surveillance of the AVH. Molnar told me in 1951 if I could help him sell a large amount of gold, he would be able to smuggle the three of us, namely a certain "Mr. Tottosy," Molnar and myself, into Austria, by truck, via Veszprem. That is how and why we met

twice in a private room of a pub on Bajcsy Zsilinszky Endre Avenue. I knew your name, but you did not know mine. I supposed the gold pieces Molnar gave me which I sold to a confectioner — originated with you.

Everything was prepared, Molnar gave us the date for departure, when I was suddenly drafted. I left word for Molnar that I had to report in 24 hours. I did not want to take the chance of being charged with desertion which meant a minimum 15-year sentence.

The next thing I knew about any of you was in Veszprem where I was confronted with both of you. Molnar confessed to the AVH our intention to cross the border, but he said nothing about his relations with the American Embassy, or about the gold. The AVH did not even ask me about those.

They kept me in solitary confinement, in the cell next to yours. I knew it was you because several times you "wanted to talk in the Parliament." I heard you attempt to hit the guard's head with a messtin, several times I listened to noises of fighting, then the slamming of the cell-door, and soon after the voice of our AVH interrogator: "Please, stay quiet, Tottosy, don't yell, Tottosy."

I was taken to the prison in the Castle of Veszprem and finally ended up at the one on Marko Street in Budapest. My trial took place in the Marko Street Court, as far as I can remember, in December. Only Molnar and I were present. *No-one mentioned you.* I never heard about you again. I have not seen Molnar since. Then next time I saw you again was here, in Copenhagen, in 1961.

This is all I can recall. It was such a long time ago. I have forgotten many of the details. If you have any more questions, feel free to ask. Excuse the mistakes, but it is difficult to write a Hungarian letter on a Danish typewriter.

Wishing you good health, I send you my warmest greetings.

Joska Rath

Josef v. Rath
Aadalsvej 14
2720 Vanlose
Denmark

Made in the USA
Columbia, SC
25 February 2023